THE 4 HOUR MILLIONAIRE

Julian Bradbrook

Disclaimer

Contents

INTRODUCTION

Welcome to the 4 Hour Millionaire where I will equip you with the knowledge, skills and resources to quickly achieve your goal of $1,000,000. Yes, that is right. I will be showing you how to increase your wealth to one million dollars.

Many people will have the dream of building themselves a pot of one million dollars cash in their bank account but only a select few will ever achieve it. The people who manage to reach this goal are the ones who have a plan in place to make it happen. I want to make you one of the people who have such a plan. Study the step by step information I give you and put it into action. You must put it into action otherwise nothing will ever change.

The 4 Hour Millionaire is based on investing in shares with a simple technique to spot the shares which will jump in value. Combine this easy to follow method with your willingness to take action and you are well on your way to one million dollars in your bank account.

Just take a moment to think about what it would be like to have so much cash. How would you feel? What would you spend the money on? Would it be a big house? A dream car? Fabulous holidays? Retire early to a tropical holiday lifestyle?

Whatever your dream is, try to take a moment now and picture it in your imagination. This image will help focus your attention to make sure you take action and start your journey to your final goal. Try and make the image as clear as you can in your mind. What are the sounds and smells that surround you in your ideal dream image? What dream possessions are around you? Who is close by you? The more real you can make the image, the more chance you have to succeed.

Now that you know what you want the one million dollars for, let's start looking at how to get your hands on it.

The plan is called the 4 hour millionaire for a simple reason which I will now explain. Trading in shares can take a great deal of time, knowledge and experience but I have devised some simple methods to cut these down to the minimum.

The method I will reveal to you is something I have called Express Share Picking or E.S.P. for short. These initials can also stand for Extra Sensory Perception and that is no coincidence. Once you have mastered what I show you with Express Share Picking, people will believe you have Extra Sensory Perception when it comes to picking winning shares as you will do it so quickly.

Using Express Share Picking you will find a share which is about to jump in price, buy it, wait for it to increase in price then sell it and bank the profit.

On average, and after you have had some practice, you should be able to pick a winning share in three and a half minutes. Buy it in fifteen seconds. Sell it in fifteen seconds. This gives a total of four minutes. I have not counted the time for the shares to rise in price as you will not have to do anything during this time except check the share price now and then.

Taking the average of 4 minutes to find, buy and sell a share and completing 60 such trades will add up to just 4 hours of action time. Can you give me a commitment of 4 hours of action to receive one million dollars?

I mentioned that you would complete 60 trades and this is all that is required to achieve one million dollars if you begin with seed capital of $10,000. If we assume you start with $10,000 and you achieve 8% increase in share price for each trade then 60 trades will mean you have reached one million dollars.

The chart below shows how your money will grow using the assumptions above. For each trade, you invest the proceeds from the previous trade. This means that you are employing the wonder of compound interest which helps speed up the growth of your money.

Seed Capital $10,000
Share price increase each trade 8%
Number of trades 60

Trade	Value of Fund
1	$ 10,800.00
2	$ 11,664.00
3	$ 12,597.12
4	$ 13,604.89
5	$ 14,693.28
6	$ 15,868.74
7	$ 17,138.24
8	$ 18,509.30
9	$ 19,990.05
10	$ 21,589.25
11	$ 23,316.39
12	$ 25,181.70
13	$ 27,196.24
14	$ 29,371.94
15	$ 31,721.69
16	$ 34,259.43

17	$ 37,000.18
18	$ 39,960.19
19	$ 43,157.01
20	$ 46,609.57
21	$ 50,338.34
22	$ 54,365.40
23	$ 58,714.64
24	$ 63,411.81
25	$ 68,484.75
26	$ 73,963.53
27	$ 79,880.61
28	$ 86,271.06
29	$ 93,172.75
30	$ 100,626.57
31	$ 108,676.69
32	$ 117,370.83
33	$ 126,760.50
34	$ 136,901.34
35	$ 147,853.44
36	$ 159,681.72
37	$ 172,456.26
38	$ 186,252.76
39	$ 201,152.98
40	$ 217,245.21
41	$ 234,624.83
42	$ 253,394.82

43	$ 273,666.40
44	$ 295,559.72
45	$ 319,204.49
46	$ 344,740.85
47	$ 372,320.12
48	$ 402,105.73
49	$ 434,274.19
50	$ 469,016.13
51	$ 506,537.42
52	$ 547,060.41
53	$ 590,825.24
54	$ 638,091.26
55	$ 689,138.56
56	$ 744,269.65
57	$ 803,811.22
58	$ 868,116.12
59	$ 937,565.40
60	$ 1,012,570.64

You can create different assumptions if you wish to see how your money will grow. Simply use compound interest calculation to show how your money will grow for various different values of seed capital, share price percentage increase achieved and number of trades.

To calculate compound interest, use the formula below

$$M = P \, (1+i)^{\,n}$$

where
M is the final amount achieved
P is the principal seed capital
i is the share price percentage increase
n is the number of trades

You can find many sites on the internet for working out compound interest simply by inputting your figures rather than trying to work out the mathematics yourself.

To give you some idea about how different values can change the final outcome, I have worked out some different options for you below.

Seed capital $10,000
Share price percentage increase 5%
Number of trades 60
Final amount achieved $186, 791

Seed capital $10,000
Share price percentage increase 10%
Number of trades 60
Final amount achieved $3,044,816

Seed capital $5,000
Share price percentage increase 5%
Number of trades 90
Final amount achieved $403,651

Seed capital $20,000
Share price percentage increase 3%
Number of trades 50
Final amount achieved $87,678

Seed capital $15,000
Share price percentage increase 6%

Number of trades 80
Final amount achieved $1,586,939

Seed capital $25,000
Share price percentage increase 8%
Number of trades 50
Final amount achieved $1,172,540

During you training, I will also show you how to place a stop loss on your trades so that if the share price drops, the shares will be sold automatically without you having to complete the trade yourself. This tool guarantees that you will not lose much money when a share price does not perform as you had predicted. It does happen so it pays to have the knowledge of the stop loss tool to keep you on track. Pay close attention to that lesson.

I will also show you how you can practice as much as you like with real share prices but without risking any money. This is a great way of learning how to use your new skills and improving them before you are ready to trade for real. The way to practice is to use free online portfolio tools where you can buy and sell shares in a virtual environment but more about that later.

Take time to study each lesson carefully. All the information I will give you is formatted to give you the required knowledge and skills in the shortest possible time but with enough depth so that you fully understand what you need to do and why.

INVESTMENT BASICS & BACKGROUND

Being a winner is never about luck

Have you ever noticed how some people always seem to come out on top? Perhaps your neighbour sold his house just before the property market downturn. Your work colleague was awarded the promotion that should have been yours. The young reality show star with very little talent now has a prime time series. The person in front of you in the lottery queue won a million.

There really is no explanation for such events other than luck: being in the right place at the right time. Or is there? Have you ever considered that life's winners, whilst appearing to have all the luck, might actually have worked long and hard at 'being lucky'?

Your neighbour might have spent hours upon hours studying the rental and buyers' market before taking the decision to sell. He may even have been an estate agent or property developer in years gone by. Your work colleague may have taken the time to figure out a cash burning problem that's been bugging management for months, or perhaps he was taking night classes in leadership skills. That young reality star: could it be that she spent years in drama school, and merely 'played a role' in the reality show? And what about the lottery winner, did he have… okay - some winners are just born lucky.

It's the same in the investment world. Some stock pickers seem to do no more than put a pin in a list of stocks to be able to pick a winner. In reality, of course, such an approach will only lose you money in the long term. Run your finger down a list of stocks and stop on a likely sounding company and you may, just like the lucky lottery ticket holder, select a winner. But do it over and over and you'll hit a lot more losers than winners. Eventually you'll lose your starting stake.

Clearly, the investor or share trader that picks winner after winner so easily has some method or system that has been taught to them, or perhaps even self-learned, through a long period of time. This is the reason why most people who have money to invest leave it to the professionals. But is that really such a great idea?

The conventional wisdom of investing

If you've ever sat down with a financial advisor, you'll have been told that there is only one way to invest. You'll have spent several hours with the advisor for him to tell you this. And he'll have asked a whole bunch of questions to 'get to know you better' so that he can tailor his investment advice to your needs.

He will also have told you about the performance of different assets over the longer term, and how shares have outperformed all other investment assets over the last 50 years and more. Which is great, of course, but I expect you don't want to invest for 50 years.

Having told you what a wonderful investment that shares are, the advisor will then tell you about diversification. He'll explain that assets tend to move in different directions, and that, for example, when shares are in a slump fixed interest investments tend to do well. So he'll advice you to spread your investment across several assets. That way when one underperforms, another will outperform and make up the loss.

The next thing he'll talk about when discussing your investments is how, perhaps just as importantly as diversification, the length of time you stay in the market will be a major factor to your performance.

In short, conventional investment wisdom says that you should diversify your holdings across all assets (knowing that doing so will mean you have losers in your portfolio as well as winners) and invest for the long term (knowing that shares have outperformed other assets over the long term).

The conventional wisdom of investment already seems something of a contradiction in terms.

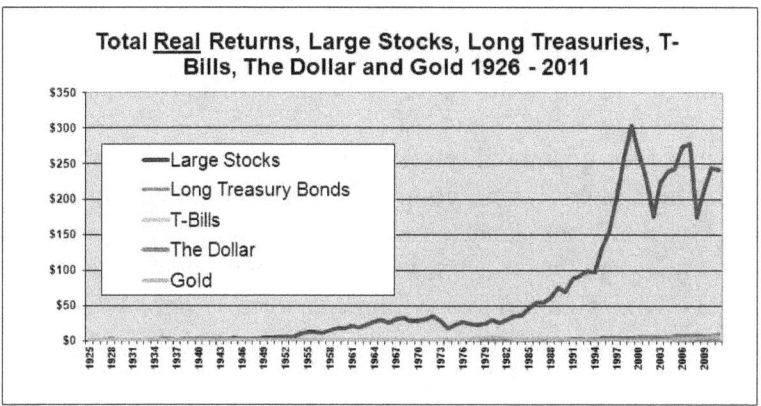

Total **Real** Returns, Large Stocks, Long Treasuries, T-Bills, The Dollar and Gold 1926 - 2011

But how does the advisor then recommend you invest your cash? In a handpicked basket of shares, bonds, and commodities? No, he'll recommend that you purchase shares in a fund where investment professionals actively manage deposits, buying and selling shares across a wide spectrum of companies.

The truth about investment funds

For the best part of the last 100 years, stocks have produced an average 10% return each year. There have, of course, been years when this return has been negative, and other years where the return has been way more than 10%. But with an average of 10% rise year on year over the long term – remember the long term that the advisor tells you to invest over – it would be fair to assume that an average equity fund should perform in line with this.

So let's have a look at the reality of professionally managed funds.

According to Goldman Sachs's David Kostin, in a report released in 2013, 80% of large cap mutual funds in the United States underperformed the stock market – in a year where it probably would have been possible to put a pin in a list of stocks and pick out a winner. Perhaps worse still, 67% of all mutual funds fell short of their benchmark index. That means that most property funds underperformed property stock performance, most transport funds underperformed transport stock performance, and so on.

Long term average annual returns on actively managed mutual funds in the United States actually lag the average benchmark return. But that's not because fund managers are poor at their job. Just like in any other industry, there are good managers and bad managers. Understanding why funds perform so poorly will help you to understand the futility of investing in collective investments schemes over the long term – or any other term.

Fund managers have to be paid, and they are paid whether the investments they manage perform well or not so well. There are dealing and administration costs on top of the fund manager's salaries (and bonuses), and then there are front end fees. Perhaps the best way to show this is by an example.

Let's say that you had $100,000 to invest. Many funds levy an upfront charge of as much as 5%. So of your original capital of $100,000, you could be investing just $95,000.

If the fund you've invested in rises by 10% at the top line, this means you're down by $500 on your original investment. That doesn't sound a lot, but compound that over 20 years and you'll be down by over $33,000.

But then you need to take into account the fund management costs, which are typically around 1.5%. And the administration and trading and settlement costs (did you know the average managed fund turns over 60% of its holdings annually). When all this is added together, there's a further chunk to come out of your annual return every year. In fact, according to the ex-CEO of Credit Suisse Asset Management, David Norman, all these extra costs add up to a real average of nearly 2.8%, each year, every year on actively managed equity funds: even if your fund loses money. Highlighting that the basis of fund costs is pretty much the same around the world.

If you take into account these charges, fees, and management costs, then the cumulative effect on that original $100,000 investment over 20 years is a colossal $291,140. Your $100,000 would have grown to $672,750 without all of these costs. But after the industry has taken its cut of your investment you're left with just $381,609.

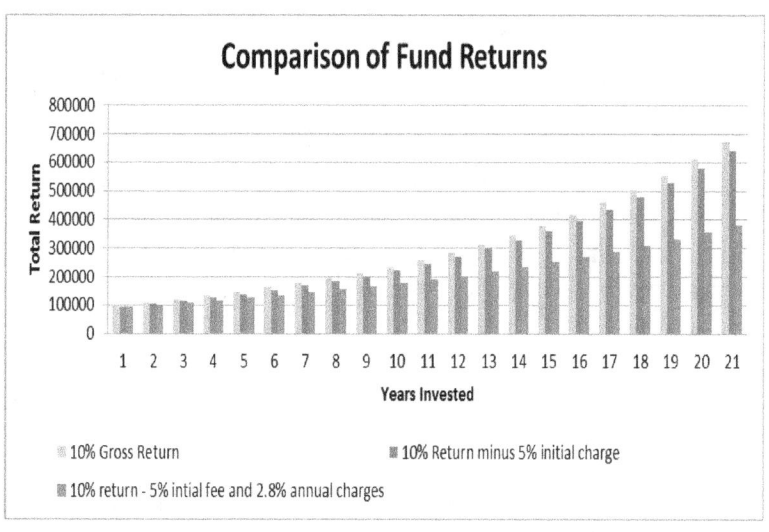

Given these facts, would any savvy investor deposit his cash into actively managed funds? Here's what John Bogle has to say about this state of affairs (he's the founder of Vanguard, one of the largest fund management firms in the world):

"The financial system has consumed 60% of the return, the fund investor has achieved but 40% of his earnings potential. Yet it was the investor who provided 100% of the initial capital; the industry provided none. Confronted by the issue in this way, would an intelligent investor consider this split to represent a fair shake? Merely to ask the question is to answer it: 'No'."

So, how do intelligent investors make their money?

Meet a few Intelligent Investors

Jim Simons founded Renaissance Technologies Corp in 1982. Over the lifetime of this fund it has made an annual average return of 30%. His philosophy is simple: he trades in easily traded securities and uses complex mathematical modelling to pick his buy and sell levels. This removes all emotion from his trades. When he buys a stock, he already knows his maximum profit and loss on that position. Needless to say, his hedge fund is one of the most active traders in the world. No long term trades here.

In 1993, **David Tepper** founded the value fund, Appaloosa Management. He learnt stock trading from his father, but specialises in trading distressed debts – the debt securities of funds that are threatened with bankruptcy. When opportunities are few, he invests in the stocks of companies in distressed industries (in the late 'noughties' he invested pretty heavily in the housing and construction industry). His fund has also returned an average of around 30% per year, with his best year in 2003 giving a profit of nearly 150%.

Joel Greenblatt invented the Magic Formula investing, and looks for value in stocks compared to 'normalized' three to four year earnings. He's very concentrated in his trading, and may have just five or six stocks positions that make up 80% of his portfolio at any one time. According to gurufocus.com, he has bought over 800 stocks in the last six months with an average return of 9.65%.

George Soros looks for value and price, with discrepancies caused by emotion and trader chaos. Where the value and price are not in synchronization, he buys and sells accordingly. His Quantum Fund has returned an average of 32% since its inception, and he's made at least 180 trades in the last six months.

Mason Hawkins has been the CEO of Southeastern Asset Management since 1975 and looks for value in companies with good people, a good business, and at a good price. When investments reach what he considers to be the right value, he sells.

Prem Watsa bought Markel Financial in 1985 and renamed it Fairfax Financial. He used the float of the company to 'do a Warren Buffet', and has a passive buy and hold strategy similar to Buffet's buying what he considers to be undervalued stock and then waiting for the return to materialize. Annualized returns are around 23%.

And then there is **Warren Buffet**, the Oracle of Omaha, and considered by many to be the investor to aspire to be. He is the master of the 'buy and hold' strategy, looking to buy into undervalued or underperforming businesses and holding them long term. Between 1965 and 2006 his Berkshire Hathaway investment vehicle produced an average annual return of 21.4%. He looks for value with price the final decider, and invests in businesses he understands. In the last six months he has bought 37 stocks with an average return of a little over 5.5%

You'll notice that these investors have a few things in common, and that there is also a couple of differences in approach, too. First the commonalities:

- Intelligent investors always have a quantifiable investment/ trading strategy;

- They look for value in their investments in comparison to

like-minded companies, and understand that value is a longer term concept;

- They also trade on price, understanding its shorty term nature;

- They are all goal focused;

- They have learned their professions.

The main difference between these investors and others like them is the time frame of investments and the number of trades they execute:

- Long term investors may hold a position for years;

- Short term investors have a more trading dominated strategy, trade more frequently, and have a more price dominated methodology;

There's one other difference that few investment advisors will alert you to. If you read through the above list again – no means an exhaustive list, I know, but indicative all the same - the intelligent investors with a shorter time frame and a strong strategy have better investments returns than the long term investors. Warren Buffet, the man who gave the world the saying 'buy when all around are afraid, and sell when all around are greedy', has made an annualized return of around 21%. The far more active Jim Simons has produced a return of 30% annualized. Nearly 50% more bang for his buck.

Before we look at the two major components of the intelligent investor's strategy – value and price - we need to consider the third, equally important piece of an investment strategy.

Trade without the emotion

Just like any commodity that can be bought and sold, share prices move up when demand is high (and/ or supply is low) and down when demand is low (and/ or supply is high). A common reason quoted by stock traders for a rise in a share price when there appears to be no logical explanation is 'more buyers than sellers'.

Now companies release news all the time. Earnings reports, details of sales, new products in the pipeline, a change in top executives... the list goes on. These, of course, can all be reasons for a share price to move in either direction. News affects the perceived value of a stock, and the market reacts accordingly.

Sometimes, though, what appears to be a good earnings report, for example, could send a share price down. Why? Most commonly this might happen when the profit of the company, even though it has increased by a goodly amount, has not lived up to market expectations – last year the company made 10c per share and this year it has made 18c per share. But if the market was expecting 20c per share, then the share price may very well fall. Market sentiment has turned against the stock.

And it is this market sentiment that is often the unquantifiable component of stock prices.

Let's consider a bull market. Prices are roaring, at multiple year highs, perhaps. Valuations – which we'll talk more about in the next section – are way above long term averages. But still investors keep piling in. Why? Because they feel good. Shares are going up, and when they are rising the natural inclination is to join in. This is market euphoria. When that euphoria reaches such a height that stock prices are rising to excessive valuations, it's often called a market blow out.

Now let's think of a bear market. Prices are falling. No one wants to buy: everyone is looking to sell their stock. The market is

25

unloved, and unwanted. Eventually there comes a time when investors, in despair at the slow bleed of losses, will sell at any price. Then the market drops even more rapidly. The final leg of a bear market is often indicated by a final fall – most commonly after a rally in stock prices (a relief rally) – which sends shares to highly undervalued levels. This is called market capitulation.

In both cases, stock prices overshoot and undershoot sensible valuations. Market sentiment has gathered such a head of steam that investors trade on this sentiment more than logical valuation. Sentiment helps to drive prices, and this gives stock traders opportunity. But you should never confuse sentiment with emotion. Where trading with or against sentiment gives opportunity for profit, trading on emotion will only cause losses.

Think for a couple of moments about the investor in a bull market that buys a stock because he wants to profit from the market's continual rise. He might have conducted his research and decided that the fundamentals for the stock's rise are good and string. For a couple of days his trade looks good but then the market turns, seemingly for no reason (other than 'more sellers than buyers'). He sits on his position, believing that the falling price is no more than a blip.

But then it keeps on falling, and his position turns to a loss. He decides to hold on. The market will turn, he reassures himself. The reasons why he bought the stock in the first place haven't disappeared. But the stock keeps on falling. Now he's in a deep loss. Eventually he can take no more. He's at that point of despair at his losses. He can see nothing but further losses mounting up. So he sells. Just before the share price begins to recover.

His original trade was made on the right basis. He researched the stock and decided it was still a buy, despite the price movement over the past few months. But then he made a fatal mistake. He traded with emotion, and failed to believe that he might be wrong. He fell in love with his position. When the market fall really began hurting, he fell out of love with his position, and he sold. He traded with emotion, both ways.

If you trade with emotion, you're going to get killed in the market. Don't ever confuse market sentiment with trader emotion.

Avoid the emotion – set a strategy

The only way to ensure that you trade emotion free is to set a strategy. Know your entry and exit levels, and then stick to them. Sure, be prepared to be a little flexible in the application of the strategy, and adjust it to suit altering market dynamics. But never lose sight of a strategy, and never fall in love with a position. If your strategy says to sell a stock if you have reached a 20% profit, then sell it. Don't break your rules because you believe the stock will move higher still, and then see it suddenly turn into a loss.

And this really brings us full circle to where we started. Stock market winners aren't winners because of luck. They're winners because they have a strategy. They trade emotion free, and know when to buy and sell. They have a basis on which they select the stocks that they trade, and they have good risk management processes – if a trade they've made goes wrong they ensure any losses incurred won't be so great that it wipes out their profitable trades. Look at those intelligent investors again, and note all the commonalities.

And that is what Express Share Picking is. It is a strategy that can be easily learned, put into place, and then used to profit time and time again. And once you have all the strategy components in place, you'll find that you, too, will be able to run your finger down a list of stocks and pick a winner at will. You'll have extra sensory perception (ESP) because of Express Share Picking (ESP).

Section Review

- Luck is reserved for lottery winners

- Over the long term, equities have outperformed all other asset classes

- Conventional investment wisdom calls for diversification – putting you into losing stocks or assets and negatively affecting your returns

- An investment advisor will recommend you invest for the long term – time in the market

- An investment advisor will recommend you invest in diversified funds

- The majority of active funds underperform the market, and take up to 60% of the return with no risk over the long term

- Intelligent investors know how to value stocks, and use a valuation method as the basis for investment

- Intelligent investors buy and sell at the right price

- Intelligent investors trade with a strategy

- Investors who 'time the market' are outperforming those that spend 'time in the market'

- Sentiment is the unquantifiable opportunity component of price

- Emotion becomes a quantifiable loss maker

One final thing…

Just before we move to the next section, *Price versus Value*, I want you to consider the following chart and ask yourself if you would want to have bought in 2000 and still be invested today, or if you think you could have made more money by trading in and out as the market price fluctuated through time.

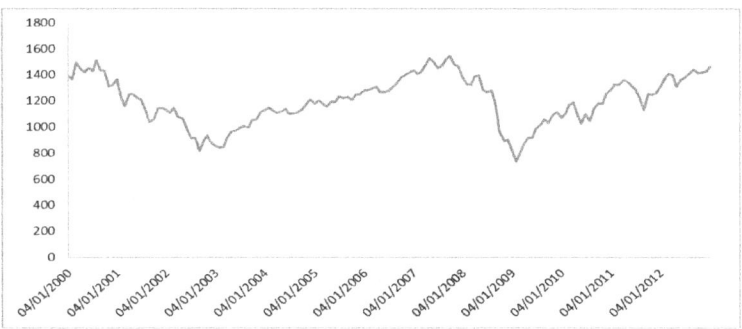

This is a chart of the S&P 500 since the turn of the millennium to the beginning of 2013. In points value, the index rose just 4.8% over the period. And yet there are plenty of traders who have made a killing through this time trading in stocks, hundreds of percentage points in profits. They haven't used time in the market. They know how to time the market.

PRICE Vs VALUE

The concept of value

One of the key things that all intelligent investors have in common, irrespective of whether they trade on a hold and buy strategy or with a more aggressive methodology, is that they all invest where and when they see value.

Too often, poor investment decisions are made because the investor doesn't understand the difference between price and value. Just because a stock has a lower share price than another doesn't mean that it is cheaper, nor does it mean that it is better value. There's plenty more to know about a company and its stock before the real value of the company can be assessed and a buy/sell directional decision made. Some analysts will spend hours, days, and even weeks researching a company before pronouncing its stock to be a buy or a sell.

You might be asking what makes me so sure that will be able to do in a matter of minutes what it takes a trained and experienced analyst so long to complete. Well, firstly you'll learn how to leverage your decision off all the analysts' work and where to quickly find all of the information you need to make an informed decision. And secondly you'll know and understand real investment value when you see it.

Perhaps the easiest way to begin to understand the concept of price and value is to consider two identical houses in separate parts of the country. A single family home in North Dakota, for example, would be priced much lower than the same home situated in the middle of New York. But just because the home in New York is priced so much higher than the home in North Dakota doesn't mean its value is more.

For example, the rental income that you could get in North

Dakota is less than that achievable in New York. But if I told you that the percentage of your outlay was exactly the same, then it could be argued that the value of both properties is the same, even though the price is so different.

It's all about the price

Okay, we're going to build the Express Share Picking Strategy based on an evaluation of a stock's value. So it may sound odd that I first of all tell you that it's all about price. But think about this for a moment, and think about what price really is.

The one thing that you'll be able to say about price straight away is that it is an easily measured commodity. If you have $10 in your pocket, then you'll be able to afford that $10 lunch. But the one in the diner next door, priced at $15… well that's one you'll have to forego.

Just like any other commodity, a stock's share price is a function of supply and demand. The more buyers there are, the higher the price will move. But what affects the way that stock investors act in the market? What makes traders buy and sell shares?

There are a number of factors that affect a stock's price. Let's leave fundamental and technical factors out of the equation for the moment (don't worry, I'll get to them soon enough), and talk about the more common factors that affect stock price.

What do you think would happen to stock prices, for example if the President of the United States was assassinated, or if there was a massive terrorist attack on New York, like the tragedy of 9/11?

You see, political and economic news, wars on foreign soil, a whole host of events anywhere in the world, affects traders' views of the stock market, and often this causes swings in stock prices that are out of sync with the real world. If the President is assassinated, does that mean that business will suddenly grind to a halt? Emotionally the world stood still after 9/11, but the wheels of industry kept turning.

News changes trader sentiments, and stock prices are, at least in part, sentiment driven. In fact, with the easy access to stock markets around the world that is now available, this change of sentiment has an even larger impact than it did, say, 20 years ago.

Understanding the emotional, sentiment driven and short term nature of stock prices is your real advantage in the market.

Value is comparative and long term

So price moves short term, and often without heed to the one thing that we, as investors, should be buying: value. You don't buy price, you buy value. Let's look at those homes in North Dakota and New York again.

I previously said that both homes paid the same amount in rental yield: let's say 5%. Now, if the home in Dakota was priced at $100,000 then that would give you an income of $5,000. And if the home in New York was priced at $1 million, then your income would be $50,000.

But what if the price of homes in New York collapsed for some reason? Would the people living in the region suddenly leave? Would businesses fail, stores close, and restaurants shut their doors? The answer is probably not. There would still be the same demand for housing, and the amount of rent paid would remain the same. But if those home prices had fallen by 25%, to $750,000, then the rental yield would now be nearly 7%. Putting it this way, what now looks better value: the home in New York, or the home in North Dakota?

So when you think about the value of stocks, you must think comparatively.

Let's take two companies, both of whose stocks are available to trade on the stock market. Company A makes $5 million a year and its stock trades at $1. Company B makes $5 million and its stock trades at $2. On the face of it, stock B might look overvalued in relation to stock A. But profit and share price is not the whole story.

Let's say that Company A has 5 million shares issued (outstanding). The value of the company is $5 million (5 million shares x $1). Company B, on the other hand, only has 1 million shares outstanding, meaning that its value is just $2 million. In other words, you could buy the same amount of profit for less than half the price. You now have a basis for a comparative valuation.

Now, let's imagine that war has broken out in the Middle East. There's an oil shock coming, America sends troops along with a handful of allies. The stock market is likely to go down across the board, and possibly by quite some way (though oil companies might fare better).

But companies A and B are both food retailers. They'll be selling to the public for as long as people need to eat and drink. Their stocks, though, get caught in the crossfire of sentiment and prices fall. But let's forget about the stock price for a moment or two. Tell me, has the real value of the company changed? Just because of war thousands of miles away, does this necessarily mean that companies A and B will make less profit?

Now you're beginning to see that value is long term, and price is short term. When the short term price falls below the long term value, the intelligent investor will buy. And when that price rises above long term value, he'll sell.

Your opportunity

If you ignore share price when considering the real worth of a company, you'll be able to calculate what a fair price for its stock is. There will be three outcomes to any such calculation: stock is either overvalued (the price is too high), or undervalued (the price is too low), or fairly valued (the price is right).

Something else to understand at this point is that markets are inefficient. They work, and they work well. They give investors and traders a place to buy and sell shares, with a huge amount of information to employ and make informed investment decisions. But if they were efficient, then all prices would at all times be priced at a fair value. But they are not, because emotion and sentiment take hold.

Buy low, sell high

An amazingly simple concept and it is how, as an investor, you'll make all your money. Too many investors, however, are dictated by human psychology and allow their trading decisions to be forced by emotional attachment. When stocks are rising, investment emotion will tell you they will always be so. Similarly, when markets are falling through the floor, you may feel like the end of the world is nigh and want to sell. It's these emotions – often voiced in terms of greed and fear – that too often cloud good investment judgement. It is the reason that causes markets to overshoot on the upside and undershoot on the downside.

On any logical and mathematical basis, buy low and sell high is the obvious investment strategy: psychologically, though, it's one of the most difficult edicts to stick to.

Become emotionally detached from your investment, look for stocks that are undervalued and sell them when they are overvalued.

The question now, is how to value stocks so quickly that you trade with extra sensory perception? And that brings us to how stocks are valued in the market today.

Valuation Methods

The whole point of determining a fair value of a stock is to determine whether it is a buy, sell, or hold. Now, of course, there are other ways to choose where to put your investment money. For example, the old man who sits in the corner of the bar you go to after work used to work in the stock market. He's bound to know what he's talking about.

You might also use a 'sweepstake' method, putting the names of likely candidates into a hat and picking one out at random. It worked when you wanted to bet on a horse in last year's Kentucky Derby, so it must have some merit, right?

There is also the tip you could read in the stock columns of the daily newspapers. But don't expect to read any thoughts or views about the tipped stock for weeks or even months to come.

If you follow any of these three methods, now and again you'll pick a winner. The law of averages says that. The Express Share Pickling system, though, uses a far more scientific and logic based approach than simply picking a name out of a hat. Not only that, but it's a method that you'll easily understand, and with a small amount of practice will be able to master.

The aim of ESP is to pick winner after winner, and not rely on the odd big gain counter balancing a string of losses. As part of ESP is based upon stock valuation it's worthwhile spending a little time getting to know how stocks are valued by investors and traders, because you'll be combining both to achieve killer results.

Fundamental analysis

When all the highly paid analysts at big city investment houses conduct their research into stock values, they will compare one stock against another within the same industry, probably even the same niche of that industry. He'll use the most up-to-date information, speak to company management, and analyse all the facts and figures at his disposal to do so. He's trained to do this, will have at least a Masters' Degree, probably in financial accounting or similar, and will use everything at his disposal to form an investment recommendation.

Fundamental analysis is about the financials of the company – the sales it makes, its profit margins, cost base, cash flow, earnings, and so on. As you can imagine, this is a complicated job, and to make it easier for people to understand what is happening at any particular time within a company and its finances, an analyst will combine all this data to produce a set of standard financial ratios. And it's these numbers that can then be used to compare one stock with another as well as measure a company's relative current financial performance against its historic results.

Now an analyst may also take into account other considerations, such as the external influence of political climate, economic outlook, up-coming changes in laws or regulations, even geographic influences, particularly in the case of the large multi-nationals.

Fundamental analysts will take one of two main approaches to the science of stock analysis. They'll examine on a top down basis, placing greater emphasis on the economy, then business sector, and finally individual stock, or they will take a bottom up approach where the order of importance placed upon these three factors are reversed.

Fundamental analysis is a science that understands markets can move by a significant amount every day, but that all of this stock price movement is no more than the background noise to the bigger picture. For this reason they largely ignore the sentiment, fear, and greed that dictate stock prices on a daily basis. Fundamental analytical outlook is long term in nature, and stock and directional trades are made easily by comparing the ratios and calculated numbers I spoke about a little earlier.

In the next chapter we'll look more closely at these ratios and what they really mean to you as an investor. But right now it's time to take a brief look at the second strand of stock analysis.

Technical analysis

I know this may sound contra to all conventional investment wisdom, but pure technical analysts really couldn't care less about a company's finances, or future growth potential. What they are concerned about is the noise that fundamental analysts want to ignore: the day-to-day price movements dictated by market sentiment and the flow of buy and sell orders.

Technical analysts use historic price and trade volume data to build up a picture of price patterns that they then use to predict future price movements. Chartists plot price changes on a graph in the form of bars, lines, and candlesticks, and often accompanied by indicators that give buy and sell signals.

This price patterning is so precise in its nature that some traders will make buy and sell decisions on a minute –by-minute basis, with multiple screens flashing away in front of them. Investment outlook, when driven by technical analysis, is much shorter term in its profile.

Other technical analysts use standard formulas of their own to help them, applying a mathematical calculation measuring stock price and rate of change to come up with a volatility number, relative strength numbers, moving averages and regressions.

Again, we'll look at some of these in some detail in a later chapter.

The power of value and price combined

Express Share Picking combines the long term valuation methods used by fundamental analysis with the shorter term price/ direction signals created by technical analysis in a truly unique way.

Investors buying for the long term are not concerned by the short term price oscillations of the market. Because they are buying stock for months or even years, there is far less concern about a short term movement that sees the stock price fall by 4% or 5%.

Technical traders, however, want to capture as much price action as they can. Day traders, in particular, may seek to trade tens or even hundreds of times a day in order to take turns of pennies on their buy and sell executions. Momentum traders use volume and price movements to trade 'with the flow' of money, understanding that panic drives investors to sell and confidence causes investors to buy (with markets undershooting and overshooting fair values accordingly).

Imagine the power in the palm of your hand when you have the value selection criteria of fundamental analysis and the short term trading signals of technical analysis combined. You'll benefit from the value driven buyer volume created from the relative and comparative under-valuation which has itself been caused by the overselling or overbuying caused by short term market sentiment. And you'll benefit from the shorter term buy and sell signals indicated by the same sentiment that gave cause to the valuation discrepancy in the first place.

Express Share Picking combines these buy and sell signals in a formulaic manner that is easy to understand and follow. It uses the most important of the stock valuation ratios and then applies technical buy and sell signals to them, allowing you to determine the most optimum time to buy and sell.

No investor has ever traded with a 100% success ratio. No fundamental or technical analytical method is ever going to be infallible. Express Share Picking realises this, and allows you to use your own variables to suit your own portfolio size and risk profile.

Within a short time, you'll be able to select the stocks to buy and when to buy them as if you had Extra Sensory Perception because you'll be using the scientific Express Share Picking method to its full advantage. You'll have the ability to quickly identify long term comparative and relative value, while simultaneously selecting the best time to buy and sell for the profit you want.

Section Review

- Stock price is a short term phenomenon

- Stock value is long term

- Markets overshoot and undershoot because of sentiment driven trading

- Irrational price movement – or 'market noise' – gives opportunity

- Price is what you pay, value is what you buy and sell

- Value is relative to markets and company history and outlook

- Value is also comparative to like-minded companies

- Fundamental investors examine long term stock valuation

- Technical traders look to profit from repeating stock price patterns

- ESP combines both fundamental investment and technical trading parameters

FUNDAMENTAL ANALYSIS

As I explained in the last chapter, fundamental analysis is the examination of a company's financial state, using factors such as balance sheets, earnings, and revenue to calculate how well a company is doing when compared to others and also in relation to its own historic numbers.

So that investors can easily understand whether a stock is good value or not at the prevailing market price, all this financial analysis is expressed in terms of single numbers or ratios. From this point it's pretty easy for you to compare the now to the before, or one company to the market average.

Express Share Picking uses the most commonly used and important financial ratios within its share and buy/ sell directional trade methodology.

Now, it would be relatively easy to give a list of these ratios and tell you whether their comparative value points to a buy or a sell. But in order to gain the most from the strategy, then you really need to understand what each ratio means so that you can measure its impact on value.

Earnings per share (EPS)

When a company reports its earnings, it will report them in two basic ways. The first is as a total number, for example, ABC made $5 million. The second way is as earnings per share.

When a company reports its earnings, the headline number means very little if not also expressed as a per share amount. As we discussed in the previous chapter, a company that earns $5 million could actually be less profitable than a company that earns $2 million from a shareholders point of view.

When a company reports its earnings in terms of per share, it is telling the world how much of its profit is attributable to each share. A company the makes $5 million might be posting a profit of 10c per share. A company that makes $2 million may be making a profit of $1 per share.

The higher the earnings per share, the more ability the company has to pay higher dividends to shareholders. What would you rather buy – a share that priced at $1 that produces $1 profit, or a share priced at $5 that produces $1 profit?

When ranking a stock as a buy or sell, an EPS 10% above the average of market competitors ranks the stock as a buy, 10% below the average ranks as a sell.

Price to earnings ratio (P/E)

There are a couple of ways in which to view a stock's P/E ratio, but here's how I like to think of it: the number calculated by the P/E ratio simply tells you how many years it will take the company to pay back your investment were it to give all its profits back to you.

For example, let's assume that you bought a share for $2, and the company makes 10c per shares. If that level of earnings were to remain unchanged throughout the period of your investment, and it paid all 10c back to you by way of a dividend, it would take 20 years for you to recoup your original investment.

The calculation of a stock's P/E is one of the easiest to make:

Share price/ annual earnings per share = P/E

The P/E ratio is one of the most easily calculated and accurate valuation ratios to investors. Not only is it simple to calculate, but it makes it easy to compare one company to another.

But there are a couple of downsides, too.

First, some investors interpret a higher than market average P/E ratio as a good thing, indicating that the stock is seen in a good light by investors and therefore being bought with the price increasing.

Second, a stock's P/E is calculated using historic earnings. These earnings may have been biased to the upside or downside by a one off, never-to-be-repeated event – a provision for bad debts, compensation paid to customers, or the capital gain from the sale of a business subsidiary, for example. This could sway the P/E ratio to the upside or downside.

So while ESP uses the P/E in its methodology, it also makes allowance for these contradictions and complications by requiring a leeway of 25% either side of market average for the declaration of a buy or sell: 25% below market average, and ESP counts the stock as a buy, 25% above and the stock is P/E is counted as a sell indicator.

Forward P/E ratio

Using earnings forecasts, the forward P/E ratio is calculated using the following equation:

Share price/ next year's estimated earnings = Forward P/E

Again this is easily calculated and often considered a better indicator of a stock's future value because it is forward looking. Many investors will examine both the P/E ratio and the Forward P/E together when assessing a stock's current value, and that's what ESP does, too.

If the forward P/E ratio is below the P/E ratio, then the stock is rated a buy, if above the stock is rated a sell.

Price to earnings growth (PEG)

This is a ratio that aims to equalize the effect of different P/E ratios. It's a more dynamic ratio than P/E, and is calculated using analysts' estimated rate of earnings growth the company will achieve.

Simply put, the lower the PEG the more undervalued the stock looks. It's calculated as follows:

P/E / estimated earnings growth rate = PEG

The disadvantage of this ratio, like many others, is that it relies on accurate analyst estimates (earnings growth rates for this ratio). For this reason, ESP allows a margin of error of 10%. The average market PEG will include stocks where growth rates have been both overestimated and underestimated, so we count this figure as being accurate.

For a stock to be considered a buy from the standpoint of PEG, ESP looks for the stock PEG to be 10% below the market average. For it to be rated a sell the PEG should be 10% above the market average.

Price to sales (P/S)

It's not too uncommon to see a situation where historic earnings are low because of a one off payment or deduction. For this reason, EPS also looks at the sales a company makes, rather than the headline EPS figure. The equation to calculate the ratio is calculated on a whole company basis, so uses the market capitalization and total sales.

Consider a company that has a total worth of $1 billion and sales of $1 billion as against a company that has sales of $250 million and the same capitalization. Clearly the larger the sales in relation to company size the better. So a lower P/S ratio is better than a higher P/S ratio.

The formula for P/S calculation is:

Total Market Capitalization / Total Sales = P/S

Where this number is lower than the market average, ESP rates the stock as a buy, and where it is higher ESP rates the stock a sell.

Operating Margin (OM)

A company's operating margin is a good measurement of how much is made on sales before tax and any interest payments. A company that has an increasing OM over time can be generally said to be benefitting from good management. Again, it's best to compare with other companies in the same sector.

The operating margin gives a good indication of a company's finances, because it measures what the company has remaining from its sales after all its variable costs, such as wages and raw materials, have been paid out. The higher the margin, the better the quality of its sales based finances.

A company that has an operating margin of 20% makes 20c for every $1 of sales. It's usual for one-off payments that will be non-recurring are usually discounted from the calculation, making the OM a 'clean' ratio.

Operating margin (OM) = Income/ Net sales

A stock with a higher OM than the average market number is rated a buy, while a stock with a lower average is rated a sell.

Cash Flow

One of the main business killers, cash inflow comes from three different sources – operational cash, invested cash, and financing cash. Cash outflow is caused by the need to pay for operational expenses, investments, and interest.

Think about your own finances and you'll get an idea of how important cash flow is. If your employer doesn't pay you for three months, let's say, you still have bills to pay. But you may not have the cash to pay them. You've got a negative cash flow, and fall into debt.

The statement of a company's cash flow is a major indicator of company financial health. Positive cash flow will give the money to pay out dividends, or reinvest within the business to improve profits, or perhaps to buy other businesses. All of this should, in turn, generate even more cash.

For this reason, a positive cash flow indicates a buy, while a negative indicates a sell. Similarly an increasing balance on a cash flow statement indicates a buy and a decreasing number indicates a sell.

Dividend Yield

The payment of dividends is viewed differently by the two main types of investor. Those who want to benefit from a capital gain see the dividend as an unnecessary payment and would rather the cash be kept within the company or invested in cash generative businesses. But many investors buy stocks for the dividends they pay, either taking the dividend to supplement income or reinvesting it into stocks. These investors would be horrified if a company suddenly stopped paying its dividends.

For this reason, we don't use the dividend as such as an indicator of either buy or sell. But it is important to understand what mechanism the dividend performs, because ESP does use the dividend payout ratio as an indicator.

The dividend yield is simply:

dividend per share/ share price (then expressed as a percentage)

This allows the dividend to be compared easily to other income bearing investments, such as cash deposit accounts, for example.

Generally speaking, a company will seek to maintain its dividend payment or dividend yield. When a company cuts its dividend, it is usually because of falling earnings and typically will lead to a fall in the share price.

Dividend payout ratio

For ESP, the dividend payout ratio is far more important. We've seen above how companies do not like cutting their dividends. But consider if a company is paying out all of its profits by way of a dividend: if its profits fall, it may be forced to cut its dividend (leading to a fall in share price).

The dividend may be a reason to buy the stock, and an increase in dividend may be a reason to buy the stock. The lower the dividend payout ratio, the more solid the dividend is likely to be. A company that pays out only half its earnings as a dividend is better placed to at least maintain the dividend should its profits suffer a temporary setback.

To calculate the dividend payout ratio:

Divide the annual dividend by the EPS (then express as a percentage)

A payout ratio of 50% or less indicates a buy, while a payout ratio of 80% or more will be seen as a sell.

The fundamental value to ESP

Now you know something of the eight elements of fundamental analysis that the Express Share Picking system uses, what importance they have in stock valuations and how to make all the necessary calculations.

Some investors, incredibly, only use one or two of these ratios to make their investment decisions. Already, by using eight of these ratios, you will be increasing the accuracy of your buy and sell selections. Of course, it may be that you will miss out on some winning trades that others who use a more limited criteria selection will make: but you'll also miss out on the losing trades that those investors pick out as winners.

ESP not only enables you to spot better quality potential stock trades, but also ranks those buy and sell signals (a buy signal is counted as +1, and a sell as -1).

Of course, the quality of the ratios and therefore the buy/ sell directional indicator depends upon the quality of the numbers input into the formulas to make the calculations. If you're worried by this, perhaps concerned that a slip of the finger on your calculator will cause a massive discrepancy and lead you to buy stock when you should be selling, then don't be. It will be good to practice working out all these numbers and equations, but before the end of this book we'll show you where to get all the ratio numbers you need. It really couldn't be easier.

But before we do that, before we pull everything together, we need to look at the final part of the ESP system. It's time to get technical.

Section Review

- Fundamental Analysis measures long term valuation

- Ratios make valuation comparisons easier

- You should always compare ratios with those of similar companies

- A ratio is only as good as the input data

- Poor cash flow can bankrupt a company

- Dividends might put a 'floor' under a share price (but beware)

- Express Share Picking uses 8 of the most valuable and best measured Fundamental Ratios

TECHNICAL ANALYSIS

As we saw earlier, technical analysis is based upon price patterns and factors such as velocity of price change. Stock traders use historical price data to build charts and graphs to more easily spot price trends and directional pivot points – prices at which the price trend changes from falling to rising and vice versa. To understand this part of ESP, it's necessary to have a basic understanding of charting.

The Elliott Wave

At the end of the 1930's, Ralph Nelson Elliott developed his stock price theory based upon social concept (remember we spoke about sentiment being the 'unknown factor' in stock pricing?). What Elliott believed was that society moves with a crowd mentality, and that this behaviour creates a pattern of waves with a set cycle.

He applied his theories to the stock market, and found that there are three basic concepts on which it stands:

- Market cycles, like social behaviour patterns, moves in a series of waves

- These waves recur, which causes a definable pattern

- Any action is followed by a reaction

Using historic price information, Elliott concluded that the characteristics of any market cycle are very specific:

- The main trend – whether up or down – will be supported by 5 waves in the direction of the trend (the impulsive waves), followed by 3 corrective waves (see diagram 1).

- This 5 impulsive and 3 corrective wave pattern constitutes one full market cycle. However, this cycle becomes part of a larger wave (again 5 impulsive and 3 corrective waves) and then forms part of the next wave and so on and so forth.

- This underlying 5-3 pattern will be constant throughout the larger and smaller market cycle periods, though the time length of each period may change.

If you look at the following diagrams, you'll see how this builds up and how the pattern of movement becomes predictable in its own way. The top line in diagram 2 shows the big picture cycle, if you like, while the bottom two lines show the 'mini-cycles' that make up the larger cycle.

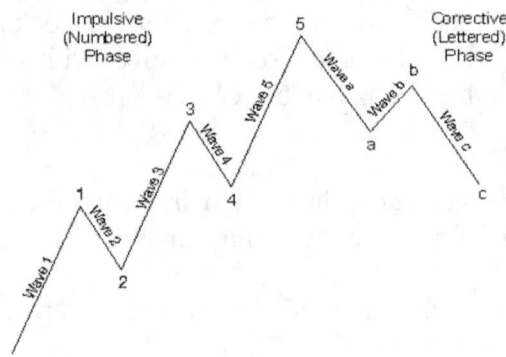

Diagram 1

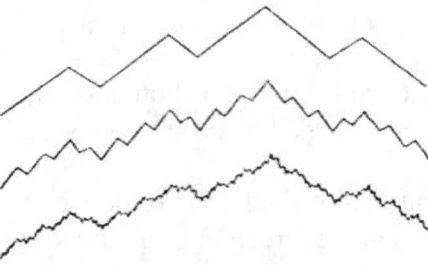

Diagram 2

54

Elliott also discovered that this market cycle moves in line with a Fibonacci sequence. Now this sequence is a mathematical enigma, and one that recurs across the natural world. You don't need to know the exact maths behind the theory, but even Leonardo Da Vinci realized its power (a examination of his most precise human studies shows that they all conform to Fibonacci numbers).

But, it is worth noting that the Fibonacci rule, when applied to the Elliott Wave says that any given value in the wave sequence is around 0.618 x the following number, and 1.618 x the number before it. So if you practice and get used to applying these numbers, you could get to predicting not just which way the market is going to move, but also how far.

Volume

The problem with Elliott Wave theory is that, as we saw a few moments ago, each recurring pattern of 5-3 builds up to a larger pattern. What this means is that when you're examining any Elliott Wave it can be difficult to spot exactly where in the cycle you are.

And so we turn to volume of stock traded to help spot market turning points and confirm trend. You see, stock price, the direction of price movement, and the speed at which the price is moving are all points of reference for spotting a price reversal, but you should never ignore the volume of stock traded. As we'll see later, there are technical indicators that use volume as a major component of analysis, with traders who use it believing that without volume no trend can be accepted as a true trend (and thus being used as the determinant of a false indication).

In general, volume increases as a trend in price is established, and it is this volume that confirms the trend to be genuine. You see, the rules of market sentiment say that as a stock price rises buyers are drawn into the market – it's a confidence thing – and this increases volume. This increased buying interest causes further buying and a cycle of price rises. The reverse is true of price falls: volume increases as a stock's price falls and more sellers come into the market.

So volume doesn't just confirm a trending price, it exaggerates it. But at some point buying pressure will ease on a rising stock price when buyers are reluctant to commit new and extra funds because the price has progressed 'enough'. When this happens in a rising market, the volume usually eases even though the stock price is still rising. So a decreased volume on a rising stock price is often an indicator of a upward trend soon to reverse.

Falling markets often show a similar characteristic before turning north, with one exception.

Capitulation, where a stock price is has fallen so far that shareholders 'give up' and 'throw in the towel' before losing any more money, sees a surge in traded volume: it's the social concept working again, with shareholders voting en masse. Capitulation will often follow a series of falls where the share price has failed to recover.

Wide spread capitulation in a bear market is an indicator that the downtrend is coming to a close, or perhaps entering a period of consolidation.

Consolidation sees prices trade in a fairly tight range before breaking out: an increase in volume at the top end or bottom end of this range is often the confirmation of the break out with the stock price moving up or down accordingly.

Stock traders don't just examine price patterns, but combine with volume to add further perspective to their price predictions. This adds to trend validation and confirmation of the stock price cycle.

Moving Average Convergence/Divergence - (MACD)

This is one of the most popular technical indicators in use today, and was first developed in the 1970's, though it didn't become so widely recognized as the invaluable tool many market chartists believe it to be. It was then that a histogram of volume was added as a further measure to anticipate an MACD crossover and a change in price trend. Confused? Don't be, it's actually pretty easy to follow. Let's start by looking at how the MACD is calculated.

On any MACD chart, you find three components. You need to know what these are called, and then we'll look at how they all interact.

- The first component of the MACD is a short time period exponential average, which is called the FASTER EMA.

- The second is a longer time period exponential moving average, called the SLOWER EMA.

- The last component is a shorter term EMA of the difference between the faster and the slower EMA's. This is the SIGNAL.

Now, it's possible to input a whole range of different time periods for the EMAs, but the most commonly used are the following:

- FASTER EMA   = 12 days

- SLOWER EMA   = 26 days

- SIGNAL   = 9 days

Because it is these time periods are so commonly used, these are the ones that ESP uses in its calculations.

When you're drawing a MACD line, you calculate the difference between the FASTER and SLOWER EMAs: this is shown in blue on the MACD chart.

The SIGNAL line – the 9 day EMA of the MACD line, is drawn in red.

The MACD is written as MACD (Faster, Slower, Signal), or, in our calculations MACD (12, 26, 9).

As well as these two lines, a histogram of the difference between the MACD and the Signal is drawn as a bar chart: there is a lot of information on the MACD chart to decipher, but it's really not as hard as you might think, and a little later you'll find out how to produce a MACD in a matter of seconds. Right now, let's look at how to use it to produce buy and sell signals.

The MACD indicators

When you compare two EMAs of different time frames, it's the MACD line that shows the trend of the price changes. By comparing the MACD line to an average, it's possible to identify a change in price direction and trend strength.

Here are the three main MACD indicators:

Crossing the Signal Line

If the MACD line crosses over the SIGNAL line, it's an indication of an opportunity to either buy or sell.

If the MACD crosses through the Signal and moves above it, then this is called a **Bullish Crossover** and is an indication of a buying opportunity.

If the MACD crosses through the Signal and moves below it, then this is a **Bearish Crossover** and an indication of a selling opportunity.

At the point where the MACD crosses the Signal, the histogram will have a zero value. It also narrows as the MACD and Signal moves toward a crossing. This movement in the histogram is what makes it such a good aid to the identification of a slowing of trend and an impending crossover.

Crossing Zero

When the MACD line crosses through zero, a move from negative to positive is bullish (a buy signal) and a move from positive to negative is bearish (a sell signal). This isn't such a strong indicator as a signal line crossover, so care has to be taken with this one.

Divergence

This is the difference between the stock price line and the MACD line.

If the stock price hits a new low, but the MACD doesn't, then this indicates that a down trending stock price could be about to reverse – in other words, a **bullish divergence**.

On the other hand, when a stock reaches a new high without the MACD line doing the same this is a **bearish convergence** and an indication that the stock price could be about to move lower.

Take a bit of time to study the MACD chart below, figuring out the MACD/ SIGNAL line crosses and compare to the changing stock price as well as the histogram, too.

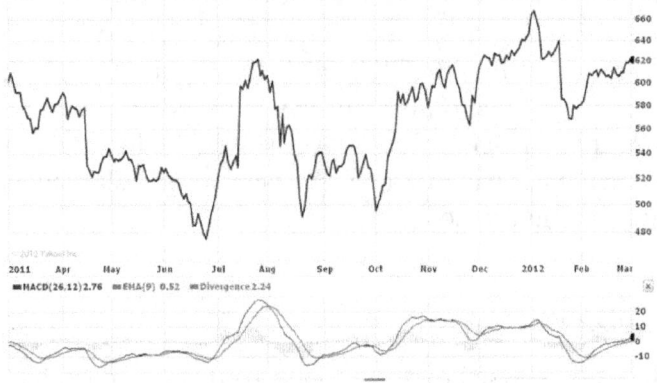

MACD is good, but not the be all and end all

Like any technical indicator, or other analysis, the MACD can give you a false buy or sell signal. So ESP doesn't use MACD as its only indicator. Also, as you'll see later, ESP also encourages you to use stop losses, which will limit any loss by a false indicator.

But as far as the MACD goes, many traders use it with a 'wait and see' process thus giving the trend change between 3 and 5 days to be confirmed. ESP combines several technical indicators so that any trend change benefits from the strongest set of indicators possible.

How ESP uses MACD

ESP rates technical indicators in a similar fashion to how it rates fundamental ratios: a buy is counted as +1, and a sell as -1. MACD indicators are therefore rated as follows:

Bullish Crossover = +1

Bearish Crossover = -1

Bullish Cross Zero = +1

Bearish Cross Zero = -1

Bullish Divergence = +1

Bearish Divergence = -1

Relative Strength Index

Have you ever heard the stock market saying 'The trend is your friend'? What this means is that when stock prices are rising (more buyers than sellers) then it's the right time to buy shares, and when they are falling it's the right time to sell. Using the psychology of the crowd, this seems a perfectly reasonable argument. But then if it were absolutely true, prices would only ever move in one direction.

Now we know that's not what happens. Prices move up and down, oscillating between the crowd buying and then selling. Over time, of course, they may move in a 5-3 pattern as per the Elliott Wave, but shorter term movements should be able to be spotted by watching what the crowd does. At least that is what the stock market theorist, J Welled Wilder, guessed in the 1970's (about the time that the MACD was being developed).

What Wilder looked at was the rate of change of stock prices, and from his studies he developed a widely used and respected direction indicator called the Relative Strength Index (RSI). This indicator is a measurement of momentum and used to indicate a trend reversal. And the best bit is, it's really easy to use.

Based on a level of 100, any value of the calculated RSI below 30 indicates an oversold position. What this means is that the share price is likely to stop falling and begin to rise. An RSI of over 70 shows the opposite: an overbought position where the upward price movement is likely to turn south and the price fall.

So, let's look at how this is calculated.

It's actually a very simple formula and is most commonly based upon 14 periods (trading days):

RSI = 100 – 100/ (1+RS)

RS (Relative Strength) is the average gain or average loss over the period, and is calculated by adding the previous 13 days' gains to the current day's gain, and then dividing this result by 14. Any losses during that period are discounted.

If the stock has fallen over the period, then all the previous 13 days' losses are added together and divided by 14. All the losses are counted as positives, and gains discounted.

If the RSI is calculated over a long period, then eventually every day's gain or loss will itself be 14 days' averages and the accuracy of the calculated number increases.

If every one of the 14 days are gains, then the RSI will be 100, and if every one of the 14 days are losses the RSI will be 0.

You could, of course, change the number of days used to calculate the RSI, which will change the sensitivity: a 10 day RSI is more likely to give an overbought or oversold value than a 20 day RSI.

Like I've said already, all technical indicators might show a false signal. The RSI is no different, but it tends to work in a slightly different way. It's certainly not unheard of for a stock price to keep moving in the direction of the current trend for a few days even when a turning point is indicated. Some traders wait for the new price trend to be confirmed before acting.

How ESP uses RSI

ESP measures the RSI is to give it a:

+1 rating if the value is below 30

+2 rating if the value is below 20

On the overbought end, we give a rating of:

-1 for an RSI over 70

-2 at a value of over 80

Bull and Bear Markets and RSI

It's only natural that you might want to consider the RSI slightly differently in bull and bear markets (a bull market is where prices are generally rising and a bear market is where prices are generally falling).

In a bull market, for example, you might consider moving the indicator levels up a notch – an overbought position might be indicated at levels of 80 and 90, and oversold at levels of 40 and 30.

In a bear market an oversold position might be seen at levels of 20 and 10, and an overbought position at values of 60 and 70.

Overall, RSI is a technical indicator that ESP adds to others when building up a fully rounded technical picture of stock strength or weakness to augment the fundamental analysis indicators we discussed in the previous chapter.

RSI and stock Price Divergence

This is an interesting concept that Wilder also noted within his technical theory.

If the share price hits a lower low but the RSI forms a higher low (for example share price previous short term low is $30 and the next low is $29, but the RSI low moves from, say 30 to 35), then this is an indicator that the recent share price fall is about to reverse.

Conversely, when a higher high is formed by the share price (say moving from a previous high of $70 to a new high of $75) but the RSI forms a lower high (say from 80 to 70), the positive share price trend is about to reverse and the share price begin to fall over a longer period.

ESP doesn't use this divergence in its calculations, because it is more qualitative than quantitative. But I've mentioned it here because it's a great warning of an impending change where you have bought or sold a position: giving a clear signal to watch the other quantifiable technical measures that we're discussing.

10 Chart Patterns to Watch

So, as we've seen and I've talked about at some length, share prices commonly trend up or down. It's impossible for anyone to say with certainty how far or for how long prices will follow whichever trend they are in. But what I can tell you with absolute certainty is that trends reverse. So what we're going to look at now are trend reversal patterns on charts.

Examining stock charts and spotting the reversal may take a little practice, but the more you do it the better you'll get, to a point where it will take no more than seconds to see which pattern is forming and use that to help you make your directional trading decision.

Here are the most important reversal patterns you'll encounter. Note how these patterns also encompass time to form and volume of trade, also.

Head and Shoulders Bottom

(Figure 1)
We're going to start with this pattern, not only because it's one of the most reliable, but it's also a great pattern for you to learn the technical terms. This gives a buy signal when the neckline is broken by the final rally in the cycle.

The Right Shoulder

After a prolonged share price fall on reasonably high volume, the righter shoulder forms when the stock price fall halts. As the price recovers, the shoulder rounds with a fall in volume. This point is the start of the neckline, and the head begins to form.

The Head

Decreasing volume is seen as the stock price falls, and then the price begins to recover with an increase in volume. The stock price rises to around the high seen on the right shoulder.

The Left Shoulder

The stock price falls again to at or around the level of the low of the right shoulder, though trading volume is usually higher than seen on the right shoulder and also the fall that formed the head.

Now the neckline can be drawn across the tops of the two shoulders. It is when the share price rises and breaks through this neckline that the trend reversal is confirmed and the buy signal formed.

A head and shoulder pattern doesn't have to be symmetrical: the time taken to form each shoulder could be different, for example. The neckline may slope slightly up or down.

It may be that once the neckline has been broken the price will fall back before rallying again. When this happens, the neckline becomes what is known as a support level rather than a level of resistance (to a higher share price).

But be warned: this formation can turn into a bear trap (one reason why we always recommend using an appropriate stop loss strategy, which we cover later).

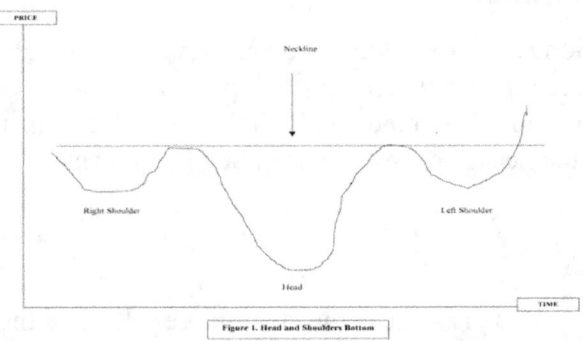

Figure 1. Head and Shoulders Bottom

Head and shoulders top

(Figure 2)

This is the opposite of the head and shoulders bottom, and would be an indicator of a reversal from an up trending price to a down trending price. Volume picks up through the time the pattern is forming.

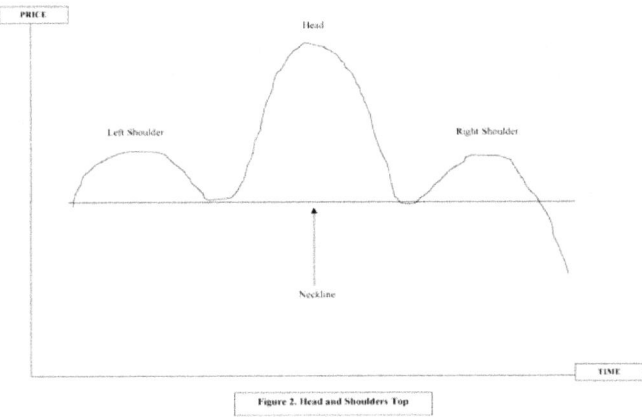

Figure 2. Head and Shoulders Top

Double Bottom

(Figure 3)

Here, you'll see a trough before a rally. Then the price falls away again to hit a second trough. These two bottoms don't have to be the same price, but will be similar.

After the second trough, the price rallies and pushes through the high seen between the two troughs to form a new uptrend.

You need to take a little care that the pattern is not part of a longer term downtrend, each step down being punctuated by a wave of buying. Its common that the bottom is what is called a 'fake bottom' and the share price will fall to new lows. Note that the longer the time between the two trough bottoms, the more likely that the trend reversal will be maintained. It's also true that the deeper the troughs, the more likely that a true Double Bottom will have formed.

Trading volume will be higher on the rally from the second bottom than the rally from the first.

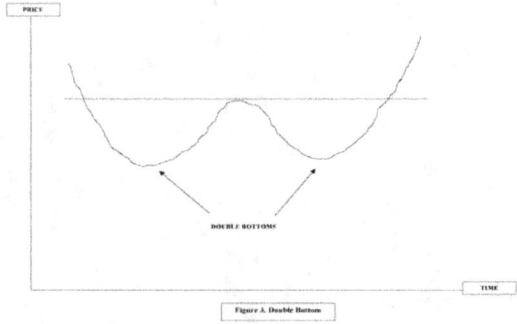

68

Double Top

(Figure 4)

If the pattern of the Double Bottom is upside down, then it's said to be a Double Top. All volume, price movement and time parameters stay in place as they are with the Double Bottom

The opposite of the double bottom, with this pattern the up-trend is reversed. After the second peak volume picks up and the price falls away. Instead of looking like an elongated 'W', the chart line will look like an elongated 'M'. Volume and time rules apply as with the double bottom.

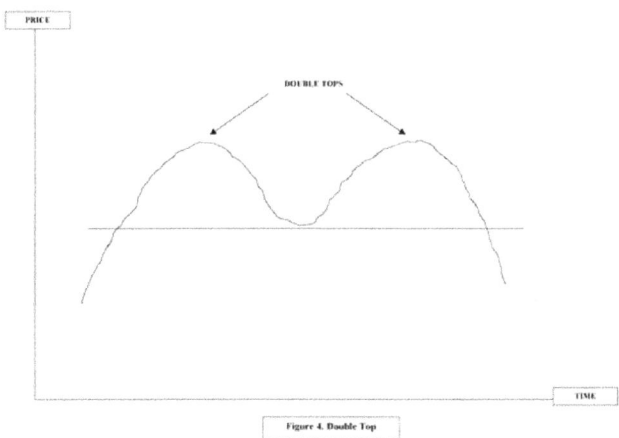

Figure 4. Double Top

Triple Bottom and Triple Top

(Figure 5 & 6)

These aren't as common as the previous chart patterns we've looked at. The troughs and peaks don't have to have commonality of size or time, so they can be fairly difficult to spot, and plenty of false Triple Tops and Bottoms are seen on stock charts. Real Triples are confirmed when the price breaks through the higher of the two peaks on a Triple Bottom, or the lower of the two peaks on a Triple Top

Real triple bottoms and tops are confirmed when the price has broken through the higher of the two peaks on a Triple Bottom (a buy signal) or the lower of the two troughs on a Tripe Top (sell signal).

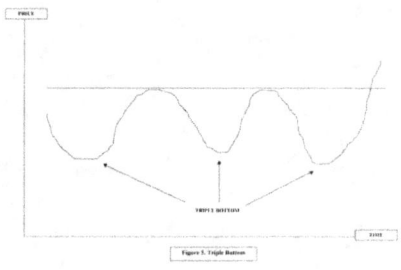

Figure 5. Triple Bottom

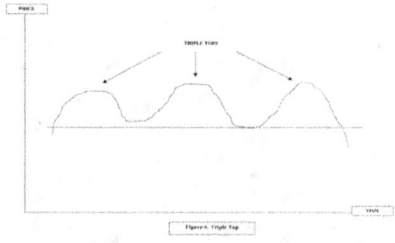

Figure 6. Triple Top

Falling Wedge and Rising Wedge
(Figure 7 & 8)

What we've really seen so far is the drawing of trend lines, though we've tended to look at one at a time (for example the 'line' drawn between two troughs or two peaks). When you draw trend lines across peaks and troughs, they can run parallel, or diverge or converge. Trend lines that converge are called wedges.

In figure 7 we see a falling wedge: when the price breaks through the upper line, then you can expect the falling share price trend to reverse (though it's often a short term reversal within a longer term trend). The time period that the wedge is formed should be no more than three to four weeks for this reason.

With a rising wedge (figure 8), the trend lines point up, and a reversal of a rising price is confirmed when the price breaks down and through the bottom of the two trend lines.

If the wedge is neither rising nor falling, then this indicates a period of consolidation with buying and selling volumes approximately even.

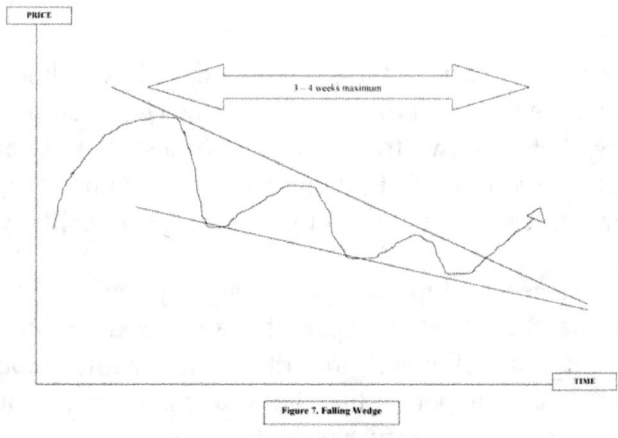

Figure 7. Falling Wedge

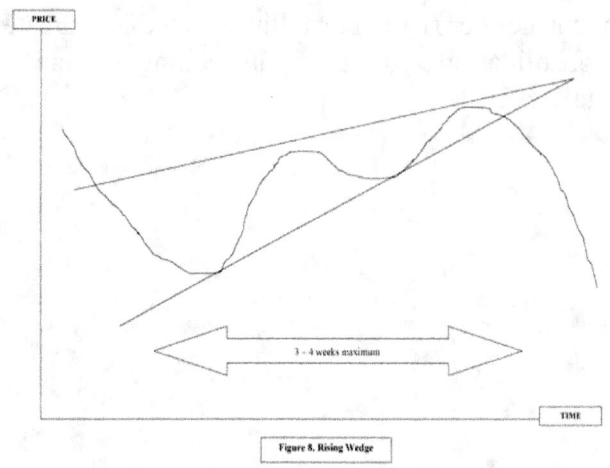

Figure 8. Rising Wedge

Rounded Bottom and Rounded Top
(Figure 9 & 10)

You could have real difficulty spotting Rounded Bottoms and Rounded Tops, but when you do you'll find them to be one of the most certain of all chart indicators. As indicated by their name, the price pattern forms a dome shape, but the real important factor is the trading volume associated with the price action.

A Rounded Bottom will see volume decrease as the price decreases, and then pick up as the price increases. With the falling price, the decreasing volume shows that selling pressure is decreasing, and with the rising price the increasing volume shows buying pressure increasing.

At the peak or trough of the Rounded Top and Rounded Bottom, the share price will track sideways for a period of time as price consolidation takes place.

The volume falls and rises similarly in a Rounded Top formation, except the increased volume after the peak is associated with a falling share price.

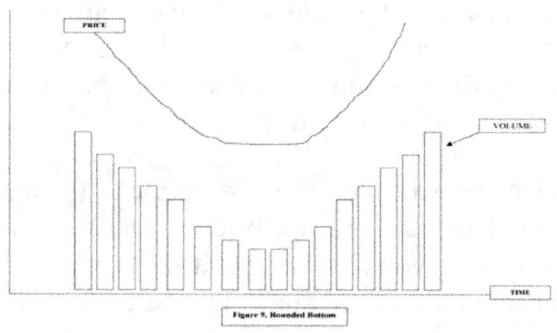

Figure 9, Rounded Bottom

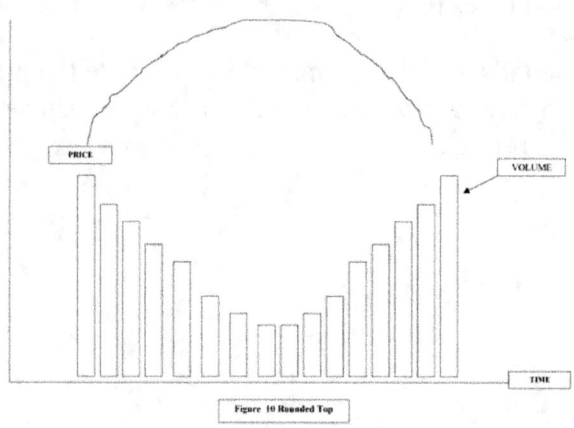

Figure 10 Rounded Top

74

How ESP uses these chart patterns

These chart patterns can be difficult to spot and take a little time to get used to. Once you do however, they can be a great confirmation tool of the fundamental analysis and technical indicators that the system uses. If you're not confident of using them or can't see the pattern forming, then you don't need to: ESP isn't just a great stock picking and directional selection system but it's flexible, too.

If you use them, however, ESP rates the chart patterns as follows:

Head and Shoulders Bottom = +2

Head and Shoulders Top   = -2

Double Bottom   = +1

Double Top   = -1

Triple Bottom   = +1

Triple Top   = -1

Falling Wedge Breakout   = +1 (but short term)

Rising Wedge Breakout   = +1 (but short term)

Rounded Bottom   = +2

Rounded Top   = -2

Candlestick Charting

You might think that all this technical analysis and charting patterns are relatively modern, and so less tried and tested than fundamental analytical practice. But you couldn't be further from the truth. Candlestick charting has been around for the better part of two centuries and it's not only followed closely because of its relative accuracy but also because it is so easy to follow visually.

To get the hang of candlestick charting, you first need to know the five elements that make up the candlestick and what they mean.

These elements are:

- Body

- Body size

- Body shading

- Upper Shadow

- Lower Shadow

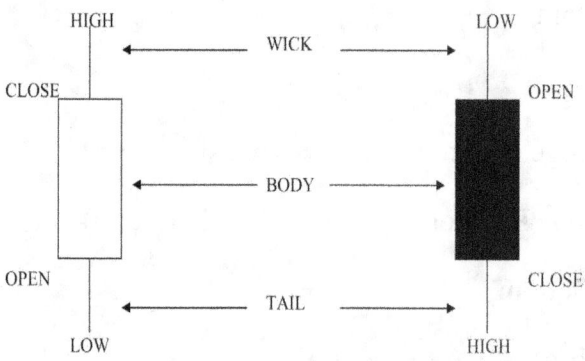

CANDLESTICK FORMATION

The Body

The body of the candlestick will either be white – depicting a higher close than open – or black – depicting a lower close than open. (some charting applications use different colors, for example green and red). The top and bottom of the body indicate the opening and closing prices.

Body length

The longer the body of the candlestick, the greater the buying or selling pressure: short candlesticks indicate a day of price consolidation.

Where a candlestick has no shadows (see below), the high and low of the stock were the opening and closing prices. A white body with no shadows shows that the open was the low of the day and the close the high. A black body with no shadows shows the reverse. (These candlesticks are called Marubozus.)

Shadows

The lines that you might see above and below the body of the candlesticks are called the shadows. The top line, or upper shadow, is called the wick (unsurprisingly, perhaps) and indicates the high price of the day. The bottom line, or lower shadow, is called the tail and indicates the low of the day.

If the candlestick has a long wick, it indicates that buyers are the dominating force, while a long tail indicates the ascendency of sellers.

If both a long wick and long tail are present, then the candlestick is known as a spinning top and shows that both buyers and sellers were active.

5 Candlesticks that indicate a buy

Bullish Engulfing

Following a number of black candles, a white candle shows that market sentiment is changing. If the white candle is larger than the previous black candle, this is called a bullish engulfing candle.

The larger the black candle engulfed, the more bullish the signal and the firmer the new trend will be.

The lower the lowest point of the white candle, the stronger the next upward movement will be when it is indicated by a bullish engulfing candlestick.

Hammer

When a downtrend hits bottom, a hammer shows the presence of buyers stepping in. The body is small, and the tail is at least twice the length of the body. There's no wick: the stock has closed at the high of the day. The body can be white or black, though a white body is considered more bullish.

Piercing Pattern

A two candle pattern where the first is black and the second white and formed in a market that has been trending down for some time. The open of the white candle is lower than the close of the preceding black candle. The black candle will be long, but the white candle longer. Finally the white candle must show that the stock closed more than half way up the black candle, and this close will be either the close of the day, or very close to it.

Morning Star

As a long decline comes to an end, a morning star is formed over three days.

The first day will be partnered by a black bodied candlestick with a long body

The second day the stock will 'gap down' – fall with a gap in price from the previous day – and the trading range will be small.

The third and final day of the pattern will see a higher close than open (a white candle day) and accompanied by a gap up from the second day's close. Finally, the close on day 3 will be at least half way up the body of the first day's candle.

The third day's white candle will have a close at least half way up the body of the first day's candle in the sequence.

Bullish Harami

This is a two day pattern, again formed in a down trending price.

The first candle will have a long, black body.

The second candle will have a white body with the open and close within the body of the first black candle.

The buy signal is confirmed by a strong third day of trading.

5 Candlesticks that indicate a sell

Bearish Engulfing

The opposite of the bullish engulfing candlestick, the black candle shows an upward trend is about to reverse. The larger the preceding white candle, the stronger the downturn will be, and the higher the highest point of the black candle the stronger the downturn will be.

Shooting Star

The wick is at least twice the size of a small body, and looks like a falling star. A black body is more bearish than a white, and this candlestick always comes at the end of a period of rising stock price. Confirmation is made when a further black candle is seen the day after the shooting star appears.

Dark Cloud Cover

A two day candlestick pattern with the second day's black candle indicating its open is higher than the previous day's close, and at least half way down the preceding white candlestick. The upward trending price should have been evident for some time, and the last white candlestick will have a long body.

Evening Star

Where a buy is indicated by a morning star, a sell is indicated by the evening star. A three day pattern as follows:

Day one has a long white body

Day two opens with a gap up and a narrow trading range.

Day three sees the black candle forms with a lower close than open and at least half way down the body of the first candle in the sequence.

Bearish Harami

Formed after a long period of rising prices, the Bearish Harami is a two-day pattern that signals a reverse to a bear trend. The body of the first candle is white, and long, and the body of the second candle is black and would fit in the body of the preceding white candle.

THE 10 CANDLESTICKS ESP USES

Buy Signals   **Sell Signals**

1. BULLISH ENGULFING   6. BEARISH ENGULFING

2. HAMMER   7. SHOOTING STAR

3. PIECING PATTERN   8. DARK CLOUD COVER

4. MORNING STAR   9. EVENING STAR

5. BULLISH HARAMI   10. BEARISH HARAMI

How ESP uses Candlesticks

Candlesticks charts are readily available from a variety of sources, and because they are so easily used visually ESP uses these to augment the fundamental and technical analysis used this far.

Bullish Engulfing, large black candle engulfed	= +2
Bullish Engulfing, small black candle engulfed	= +1
Hammer, white body	= +2
Hammer, black body	= +1
Piercing Pattern	= +1
Morning Star	= +2
Bullish Herami	= +2
Bearish Engulfing, large white candle engulfed	= -2
Bearish Engulfing, small white candle engulfed	= -1
Shooting Star, black body	= -2
Shooting Star, white body	= -1
Evening Star	= -2
Bearish Herami	= -2

We've spent a while looking at technical analysis and how all the indicators and charts build into ESP. You should, by now, be aware that even fundamental and technical analytical methods are not infallible. By combining the best indicators from both in a methodical way ESP gives you a unique and exceptionally easy-to-use stock and direction selection system. Before we see how all of the information fits together, and I tell you how easy it is to retrieve the information you need to put the system into action, let's just review what we've covered in this chapter.

Section Review

- The Elliott Wave is a 5-3 pattern

- It is based on a social concept of crowds

- Elliott Wave Theory forms the basis of much of technical analysis

- MACD uses historical pricing to predict the upcoming trend

- MACD is, like most technical analysis, a visual, easy-to-use indicator

- MACD has extra power when combined with its histogram

- Candlestick charting has been used for nearly two centuries

- Candlesticks are easy to use

- Candlestick charts have defined patterns to indicate trend reversals

- There are ten common chart patterns used by stock technicians

- They can be hard to spot and practice is needed

- It's best to use them to confirm other analysis

PULLING ALL THE STRINGS TOGETHER

Now for the fun part

We've talked long and hard about the background to Express Stock Picking, and looked at how intelligent traders make their profits. We've seen how much better the performance is of those investors that take a more active approach to their business than those more traditional 'buy and hold' investors.

There is no doubt that some traders – particularly day traders - have a natural ability to pick stocks and direction. Just like a baseball pitcher has a natural throwing arm and a champion sprinter has a natural stride. But let's make no mistake, the best traders, just like the best sportsmen and best businessmen, also have to learn their trade.

The beauty of ESP is that it uses all the information that's readily available to you, and anyone else, in a way that not only is logical and methodical, but it's also easy to use.

You now have an understanding of how fundamental analysis looks at longer term prospects, while technical analysis focuses on shorter term opportunity. ESP uses both in a unique scorecard way that makes it easy to pick winners. Then, once you've chosen the stock to buy, ESP makes it easy to monitor and take profits.

No longer will you be forced to look on as others pick winning trade after winning trade. You'll be able to use the ESP system to take advantage of publicly available information, and build a stock scorecard that tells you exactly which way to trade.

It may be that, right now, you've had a bit of information overload. Taking in all the analytical stuff that we've been through might take some time. I could, of course, have said 'here's what you do, now go ahead and do it.' But that wouldn't help you spot a trade that goes wrong – there won't be many, but no system can guarantee 100% success. If anyone tells you their system is 100% reliable, an absolutely sure fire way to beat the market every time, turn and run for the hills.

That's not what ESP is about. ESP is the system that helps you pick those winners, and keeps any losses to an absolute minimum. Before I show you exactly where to get all the information you need to build your ESP scorecard, and how you can do that at the click of a mouse, I want to talk about the importance of profit.

After all, as a wise man once said:

"Working will earn you a living. Profits will earn you a fortune. Work full time on earning your living, and part time on making your fortune"

ESP is going to give you the ability to work part time – just a few minutes each evening, or perhaps during your lunch break – to make your fortune.

The importance of taking a profit

You know, every successful trade I ever made had one of two things in common.

One of those things is profit. If every stock trade you ever make turns a profit, you'll never go bust. Now there will be get-rich-quick schemes that tell you that you don't even need to move away from your computer screen to make big money – really big money. They promise you that you don't need to have any understanding about anything, and that all you have to do is set up a website, add on a few click-to-view ads and you'll be a millionaire in no time.

Then there are those schemes that promise to make you a fortune from every 'member' or 'customer' or 'affiliate' that you sign up to sell the latest health product or fitness fad. They promise that soon you'll be rolling in the cash which others efforts are rewarding you with.

ESP is neither of these. You'll notice that I've been at pains, and gone to some lengths, to explain the mechanics behind the system. Not once have I said 'just press this button and riches will come tumbling out of this money making machine.' It's important that you understand what lay behind ESP:

- Hundreds of years of analytical expertise;

- Theories that have been tested and retested;

- A methodical approach;

- The combination of long term value and short term opportunity.

Neither does ESP claim that you'll make money from the efforts of others without putting in some work yourself. Of course you'll have to put in work. That's a given. In fact, right at the very beginning, didn't I tell you that there would be work involved? In fact, the title of this book gives it away. Four minutes: that's the work you'll need to put into every winning stock trade you make.

Back to taking profits.

One of the beautiful things about ESP is that it allows you to take the amount of risk that makes sense to you. When we discuss the ESP scorecard you'll see exactly what I mean. But it also allows you to set the profit levels you want to make.

Now let me tell you about profit levels in stock trading.

The average gain on stocks over the last 100 years has been about 10% per year. Now, that's a good amount when you measure it against the returns made on cash deposits, bonds, property, and even gold. But it will never get you to retirement early. It won't let you give your kids the opportunities you never had.

You could follow penny share guides. After all, don't they make hundreds of percentage points on some of their selections? The answer is yes. But isn't it strange how you never hear about the number of penny shares that are tipped which fall to nothing. Would you like to lose all of your investment capital on a single trade?

So let's look at the intelligent investors again. The real big and consistent winners make around 30% per year, on average. At that rate it would take 18 years to make $1 million from your $10,000 capital. That's not bad. But just imagine if you managed to select one stock every two months using ESP, and each stock gave you just 8% profit. You'd reach that $1 million in less than ten years. If you could make that one stock every month, you'd be a millionaire in 5 years. Yep, five years.

While you think about that, why not go and get yourself a coffee? Then take the time to read through what we've discussed so far. Because what I'm going to tell you now is the second thing that successful trades have in common. And it might surprise you to hear what I'm about to say.

Minimize those losses

The majority of my most successful trades came out to be profitable. That's because I had this strategy and kept to it. I took out the emotional pull of stock trading – and it is there, believe me - and took my profits when my strategy told me too. Now and again I sat and watched the stock I'd just sold move higher still. Was I disappointed? Did I start thinking to myself, 'if only I'd held on a little longer?' The honest answer is no, not once.

You see, there was also the flip side of the coin: those trades that lost me money. The remainder of my successful trades! Dumbfounded? Can't understand that I would consider a loss making trade as successful? Let me explain.

Obviously, I would rather all my trades were profitable. That goes without question. But I'm also long enough in the tooth, with enough experience, to understand that no one and no system is ever going to select 100% successful trades. There are too many external factors to consider. Those same factors that present the trading opportunity can just as rapidly take it away.

So any successful trading strategy always has a method of damage limitation, a system of minimizing losses when things go horribly wrong. And that's why I say that some of my most successful trades have actually lost money: not because they lost money but because they concreted the validity of the strategy and stopped those losses from destroying my larger profits. They actually prove that my whole strategy works.

A good risk management system coupled with ESP will help you realize the full profit potential of the system. The extra sensory perception of stock picking and direction selection that ESP will give you will be even stronger when you are able to accept the losing trades and quickly move on to the next profitable.

The question is how do you manage risk within ESP, and take out the emotions that you could experience and that would cause real damaging losses within any stock trading system?

Risk Management within ESP

Okay, so the first thing is this: we're going to treat your stock trading as a business, and all businesses have risk. Shop owners could have rotting produce left at the end of a day or week, or staff could leave, perhaps the electricity supply gets disrupted. But that shopkeeper will have processes in place that cuts that risk. He might have a generator on standby for emergency electric, he could run a staff lending scheme with a nearby store, and he is likely to have insurance policies covering most other areas of business risk.

Your business will be no different. Your risk management strategy will increase your profits by decreasing the chances that a single trade will ever do real damage to them.

The first thing to do is to decide how much of your trading capital you are prepared to lose on any single trade. Remember, you're on your way to making a million dollars.

I use a 5% stop. In other words, if my trade gets to a point where it's 5% down on opening value, then I sell it and move on to the next trade. Now let's think about this for a second. Every time I place a trade into the market, I'm prepared to take a risk with 5% of the money I'm investing.

Let's assume you did the same, and started with $10,000. You would need to execute over 60 losing trades in a row for your initial $10,000 to be wiped out (and that includes trading costs). Working the right balance of profitable trades against loss making trades is clearly going to keep those profits rolling onto that magical mark of $1 million.

How to use stop loss orders

Using a stop loss order is going to let you know your maximum downside on a trade even before you put the play into the market, and that's a huge comfort factor. By placing a stop loss order on your trades, you'll immediately remove any emotional tie you have to the stock or the trade itself.

And when your position becomes profitable, then you can use a stop loss order to retain those profits. Even though you'll be monitoring your position against the ESP scorecard daily, this is a must: retaining profits in a sudden and unexpected downturn is a key to remaining highly profitable.

Of course, you could use some fancy options strategy to minimize any losses, but one of the beauties of ESP is that it's easy to understand, simple to execute, and profitable.

We're going to look at the two stop loss orders that you'll be employing in your risk management of ESP.

The Stop Loss Order

The whole idea of this order is that if the trade goes wrong it will automatically sell out for you. It means that you can go about your daily business while knowing that your ESP position is not going to lose you a heap of cash. It keeps your trading disciplined, takes the emotional stress out of trading, and lets you get on with your life.

So you place a stop loss order at 5% below the price which you paid for the stock. If the stock falls by 5% from the level at which you bought it, then your position will be sold, preventing a larger loss. There are two types of stop loss order;

Stop Market Order

This type of stop loss will trigger at a limit price which you set, and then sell your shares at market. What this means is that it will place an order into the market to sell your shares at the best price available at the time. You'll be guaranteed to sell all your shares, but if the stock is moving violently lower you might see some of those shares trade below the limit price which triggered the sale.

Example

You buy 1000 shares at $10, and simultaneously place a limit stop to sell at market at 5% below your buy price.

The market is hit by a sudden shock, and the stock tanks. When the stock falls to $9.50, your order is placed in the market, but at the time these are the bids available:

500 shares @ $9.50

500 shares @ $9.40

Your stop loss at market will be triggered by the price falling to $9.50, and you will sell 500 shares at $9.50 and 500 shares at $9.40.

Stop Limit Order

Again, this order is triggered when the loss limit price is reached, but it will then put an order into the market to sell stock at the limit price. The downside of this type of order is that it does not guarantee your stock will be sold in a rapidly falling market. However, it does guarantee that whatever shares are sold will be sold at the limit price.

Example

You buy 1000 shares at $10, and simultaneously place a limit stop to sell at the limit of 5% below your buy price.

The market is hit by a sudden shock, and the stock tanks. When the stock falls to $9.50, your order is placed in the market, but at the time these are the bids available:

500 shares @ $9.50

500 shares @ $9.40

Your stop loss limit will be triggered by the price falling to $9.50, and you will sell 500 shares at $9.50 and be left with 500 shares.

The mechanics of the ESP strategy are flexible enough to let you and your attitude to risk decide which type of stop loss order you use, but you should always place a stop loss on the position which you are opening. It's easy to do, and most online brokerages won't charge unless that order is executed.

Now let's look at a way to stop your profits from tumbling by using another form of stop loss order.

The Trailing Stop Order

The aim of this type of stop loss order is to protect your profits. As we'll see in short while, as well as a known level of risk you may also have a known price at which you will want to take your profit. What you won't want to do is sit there and watch a profitable position, which may have risen to a fraction below your sell price, disappear if the market falls out of bed.

A trailing stop works similarly to a stop loss limit. It will be particularly useful to you as an ESP trader when you're monitoring of your position shows that the upward trend you correctly identified is now coming to a close. You might still feel that there is more life in the upside, but you'll want to protect your profits from dwindling should the stock suddenly turn south.

Imagine that you bought stock because ESP told you that it had a more than good chance of making gains over the next few days/ weeks. When the share price has risen, you're left with a couple of options:

- Sit tight, and hope the share price keeps rising. But then the question of when to sell arises again. ESP will tell you this, but what if the share price suddenly falls before you conduct your monitoring and decide to sell?

- Sell the shares and bank the profit. Not a bad thing, but what if ESP were still telling you the stock was a buy, and then the shares continued to move up?

- Place a trailing stop order at 2% below market. What this does is continually raise the price of the stop trigger as the price of the stock moves up.

For example, if you bought 1000 shares at $10, and the price moved up to $11, you'd be sitting on a very nice profit. But perhaps you feel the share price could progress further, to $12 or even $13. So you decide to sit on your position, but place a trailing stop at 2% below market. This means that effectively, should your shares fall to $10.78, then your position would be sold out (at market as in the stop order example above).

However, if the stock price rises further, let's say to $11.50, then the trigger price on the trailing stop rises, too (to 2% below the highest price achieved, in this case $11.27). Then if the stock falls your position will be should the price fall to or through the new higher stop limit.

A trailing stop limit gives you peace of mind when your position is in profit.

That's enough on stop loss orders now, except to say this: always employ a stop loss order as part of your personal ESP strategy when opening a position. The levels at which you place the stop loss will depend upon the risk you're able to accept on your way to your goal.

(Remember, the tighter your stop limit to the current market price the more likely it will be executed against)

How much Profit do you want to make?

There are two ways of taking profits.

The first is to decide on a set level of profit and stick to it. For example, you may decide that you want to make 8% on each winning trade. If you buy stock at $10, you will place a sell limit at the same time to sell your shares at $10.80.

Don't forget, you will also be placing a stop loss order, too. So it's important to place the stop loss and the sell limit as 'one cancels the other'. What this means is that if one of these two sell orders is executed the other will be cancelled, thus preventing two sales and a resulting short position in a volatile market.

The problem with this is that you are limiting your profits to just 8% per trade. On top of this, if the stock doesn't improve by the full 8%, then you could miss out on any profit (one reason that I recommend you also place a trailing stop when the stock moves into a profit).

The second way to take profits is to continually monitor your position, once a day after the markets have closed, and allow your profits to roll up until the ESP scorecard tells you to sell. Again, you'll be employing a trailing stop to protect yourself from sudden market shocks.

Don't forget, when you buy your original position you'll have placed a stop loss order in the market, too. Once your position swings into profit, replace that stop loss order with a trailing stop.

Now, you may be more comfortable with picking a pre-determined profit level, selling at that level and then moving on to the next stock. I prefer to let my profits run, and cut my losses. Just three or four minutes each night keeps me informed of the changing trend of my position and tells me whether I should sell or not. Meanwhile, my trailing stop gives me protection on my profits and lets me get on peacefully with my daily life.

And that gives me just the risk profile that I'm happy with. Before you put ESP into practice, you should understand what risk you are prepared to accept.

There's Attitude to Risk and there's Risk Tolerance

There is a difference between your attitude to risk and how much risk you are prepared to accept. You might realize that your investment will go up and down on a daily basis as the market rises and falls. Remember, ESP looks for value and price trends. On the other hand, you might step back at the thought of seeing a profit one day nearly wiped out the next. How you feel about the ups and downs of the market is how you feel about risk: your attitude to risk.

If you have a risk-averse attitude, then you'll probably have to settle for the meagre returns on cash deposit accounts. If you have a higher acceptance of risk, then you'll be more relaxed when seeing your ESP trading balance move up and down, realizing this is part of a bigger picture.

Risk tolerance, however, is the factor that really affects your investment profile. Tolerance to risk is all about the money, and actually has little to do with feelings (though it is often confused with attitude to risk). It is all about your capacity to suffer short term losses in the attempt to make longer term gains. If a $1,000 loss won't make a difference to the way you live your life, but $5,000 will, then that's where your tolerance lays.

This risk profiling is something that you need to consider when building your ESP strategy, because it will affect the profits you want to take and the losses you are willing to accept along the way.

And this is exactly the reason we use stop losses, trailing stops, and monitor our open positions every day: four minutes a night puts the fear to flight.

We're nearly done. You're nearly ready to begin working on your four hour million. Already you've come a long way. Now all that's left is for me to show you where to get all the information you need to put ESP into practice, and then how to build the ESP scorecard that's going to help you select those buys and sells.

Section Review

- ESP uses information readily and freely available

- No trading system is 100% fool proof

- ESP uses hundreds of years of analytical expertise

- ESP combines both long term valuations and short term price opportunity

- The average gain of US equities is 10% per year over the last 100 years

- Making just twelve winning trades per year, with 8% profit on each, will see $10,000 turn into $1,000,000 in only five years

- ESP uses stop loss and trailing stop orders to minimize losses and protect profits

- ESP is flexible to your risk profile – you can run with profits or take them at pre-determined levels, while benefiting from peace of mind

- The ESP scorecard, monitored for a few minutes each day, will alert you to an upcoming change in price trend, indicating the optimum time to sell your stock position

THE EASE OF INFORMATION

Years ago, finding all the information needed for the ESP system would have been a full time job. Not only that, but it would have been cost prohibitive, too. The internet has changed all of this. You can now access all the information you need to build your ESP scorecard at the click of a mouse and the tap of a couple of buttons on your keyboard.

You don't even need to use a spreadsheet, and certainly don't need to spend hours on collecting data, double and treble checking all the results before coming to a trading decision. I'm going to show you where to get all the information you need, and how to get it. We'll start off with the fundamental analysis.

Open your internet browser, and follow me into the free information age.

Accessing Fundamental Analysis Numbers

We're going to use Yahoo! Finance, **finance.yahoo.com**

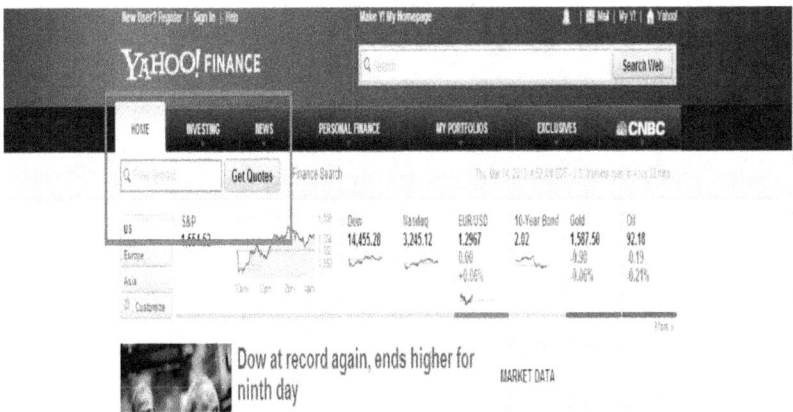

In the top left hand corner, you'll see a box to enter a stock quote. If you begin to type the name of the company you are interested in researching, then you'll be presented with a list of possibilities and you can select your stock from there. But we're going to look at Microsoft, whose symbol is MSFT. Type that in and then click on "Get Quotes".

You'll notice on the stock summary that there is a lot of the information ESP uses: EPS, P/E, etc. but what that doesn't show is a comparison to like-minded companies, and remember, that's what we want to use. On the stock menu to the left, there are a number of options. Find 'Competitors', and click on that.

Here you will find five of the eight pieces of information you need fill in on your ESP scorecard for Microsoft: Operating Margin (OM); Earnings per Share (EPS); Price to Earnings Ratio (P/E); Price to Earnings Growth (PEG); and Price to Sales (P/S). Notice that on the right hand side of the table are all the respective sector values. It's an easy task, using the ESP scorecard rules laid out in the chapter where we discussed fundamental analysis to make the comparisons needed and then write down the stock score.

Sometimes there won't be a value for the industry: in this case compare to the competitors listed, which are deemed by the market to be the company's main and largest competitors.

But that still leaves us three numbers short.

On the left hand menu, click on 'Key Statistics'.

You'll see below that you've now found the Forward Earnings Per Share, for use on the EPS scorecard.

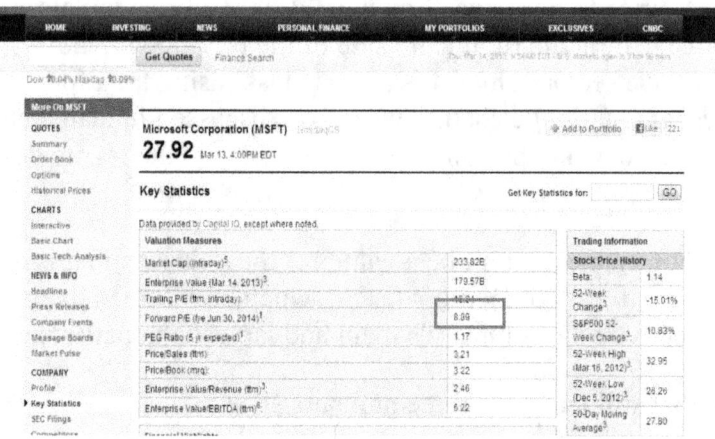

Now, on the left hand menu again, scroll down and click on 'Cash Flow', under the 'Financials' heading.

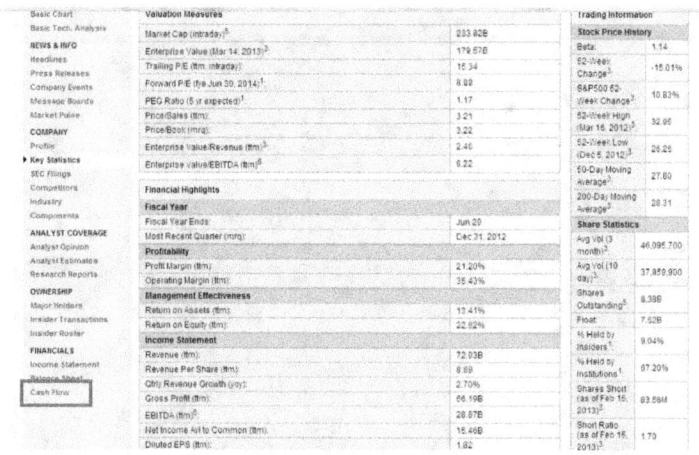

Now, as you can see here, you've found the cash flow data to use on the ESP score card:

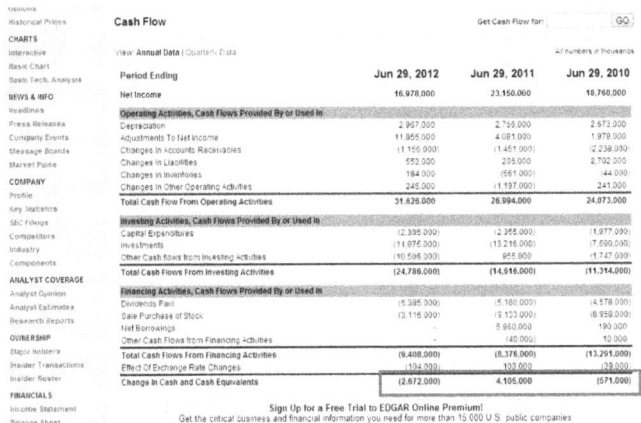

Now, it's time for some real work. Go back to the stock summary.

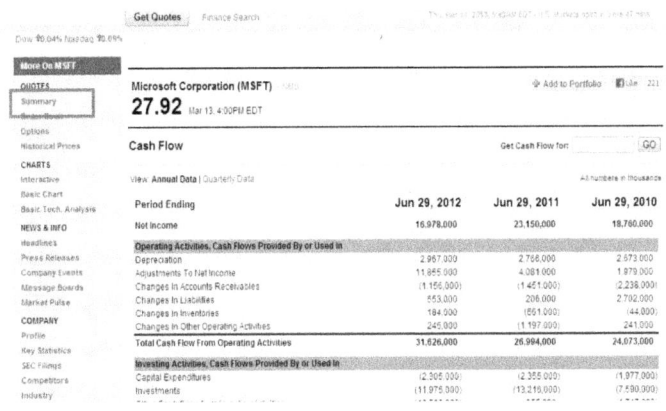

On the stock summary screen, divide the Dividend by the EPS, and then convert to a percentage (by multiplying by 100).

You now have all eight of the fundamental ratios to use on your ESP scorecard.

Now we're going to look at the Technical analysis tools you'll need. And I think the easiest thing to do is to stick with Yahoo! Finance (though there are plenty of other charting tools you could use, of course).

Technical Analysis at your finger tips

On the left hand menu, under 'Charts', select 'Interactive'.

Then, under 'Chart Settings', select 'Line Type' and 'Candlestick'.

Now, select 'Technical Indicators', and you'll see a drop box appear. In this drop box, select 'MACD', 'Relative Strength', and 'Volume'. You'll need to do this separately, and each time you'll be asked to input the data time periods (except for volume). The pre-input data should be the ones you need (refresh your memory by rereading the Technical Analysis chapter), so you won't need to alter any numbers.

When you are prompted at each step, click 'Draw'.

Finally, on the new chart, click on 6M – this will replace the one day chart with a six month chart.

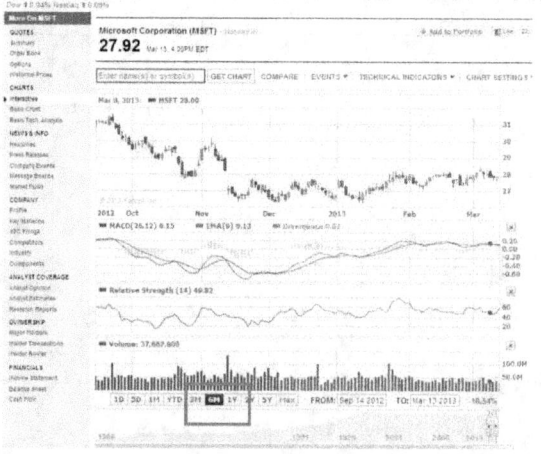

Now you have all the MACD, RSI and volume information you need to use on your ESP scorecard, using the methods discussed in previous chapters.

It really is that easy. There are plenty of financial information sites and charting tools that you can use, but Yahoo!finance is the largest and most complete you'll find anywhere. It's easy to use, fast and reliable.

All that is needed now is to have the scorecard available to build your stock buy or sell signal, and then know exactly how to use it.

THE ESP SCORECARD

Now you get to use all the information that you've taken the last couple of minutes to accrue and build your ESP scorecard. And it really couldn't be easier. ESP uses negative marking, which means every negative is deducted from the positive (many other stock picking systems simply discount the negative). This has the effect of making stock selections more bearish: in other words a buy signal has to be stronger than under some other stock trading systems.

It also uses fundamental and technical analysis, combining them uniquely in a way that other systems simply don't. As I've said several times, when ESP picks a stock as a buy it's because the price of the stock is low compared to its long term real value *and* the short term metrics are in line for a price trend reversal. It's impossible to say how fierce the reversal will be and how long the new trend will last, but by monitoring the position by using the ESP scorecard, taking just a few minutes each day, you'll be able to spot the new trend reversal before it happens.

ESP enables you to take the long view while making the most of shorter term movements in price. It's like taking the volatility out of long term long positions.

First let's look at the Fundamental Analysis Part of the ESP Scorecard.

Fundamentals		Used	Score
Earnings Per Share	EPS	1	
Below market average	+1		
Above market average	-1		
Price to Earnings	P/E	1	
>25% below market average	+1		
>25% above market average	-1		
Forward P/E	FP/E	1	
Below market average	+1		
Above market average	-1		
Projected Earnings Growth	PEG	1	
>10% below market average	+1		
>10% above market average	-1		
Price to Sales	P/S	1	
lower than market average	+1		
higher than market average	-1		
Operating Margin	OM	1	
higher than market average	+1		
lower than market average	-1		
Cashflow	CF	2	
positive cash flow	+1		
negative cash flow	-1		
Increasing cash flow balance	+1		
decreasing cash flow balance	-1		
Dividend Payout Ratio	DPR		
<50%	+1		
>80%	-1		
TOTAL			
FUNDAMENTAL SCORE (Score/ Used)			

You'll notice that every Section has a points used and a points score except the dividend payout. This is because not all stocks pay a dividend. The total maximum score will be +9 (if the dividend payout is used) and the minimum score will be -9.

A score of -9 indicates the stock is a strong sell on long term valuation, while + 9 indicates a strong buy. However, just because a stock is a strong buy on long term fundamentals does not make it a short term buy. It could be that you would buy the stock and then see the share price fall from current levels: market sentiment can be fickle. It's also possible, of course, that market insiders are selling the stock because of some information not widely known (did I really say that out loud?).

So we add the technical analysis scores into the mix to tell us if the timing of a buy is right.

MACD	Max/ Min	3 / -3
Bullish Crossover	+1	
Bearish Crossover	-1	
Bullish Cross Zero	+1	
Bearish Cross Zero	-1	
Bullish Divergence	+1	
Bearish Divergence	-1	
TOTAL		

RSI (adjust for bull and bear markets)	Max/ Min	3 / -3
Below 30	+3	
Below 20	+2	
Above 70	-2	
Above 80	-3	
(take note of RSI/ Price divergence in bought positions as a warning sign)		
TOTAL		

Candlestick Charting	Max/ Min	2 / -2
Bullish Engulfing, large black candle engulfed	+2	
Bullish Engulfing, small black candle engulfed	+1	
Hammer, white body	+2	
Hammer, black body	+1	
Piercing pattern	+1	
Morning Star	+2	
Bullish Herami	+2	
Bearish Engulfing, large white candle engulfed	-2	
Bearish Engulfing, small white candle engulfed	-1	
Shooting Star, black body	-2	
Shooting Star, white body	-1	
Evening Star	-2	
Bearish Herami	-2	
TOTAL		

Again, we negatively mark, with the maximum score being +8 (a strong buy) and a -8 score indicating a strong sell.

Notice that ESP ranks long term value and short term opportunity almost as equals. This is deliberate, and makes the ESP scorecard even more relevant to today's markets.

Simply add the two scores together to result in the ESP Buy/ Sell score. A score nearer the maximum of +16 (17 with the dividend payout included) indicates the strength of the buy signal, while a score moving toward the minimum of -16 (-17) indicates a strengthening sell signal.

When the scores are added together, both the long term fundamental score and the shorter term technical score must be positive for the stock to be a buy. This is not necessarily true for a stock to be sell: if you hold the stock, it is possible for it to be a long term buy but a shorter term sell.

Let's say you ESP Scorecard stock ABC, and your result is +12 (from 16). This would indicate a pretty strong buy signal. So you buy the stock and the price drops a little. As you are monitoring the stock you see that the ESP Score has actually risen to +14: the long term valuations remains, but the buy signal is becoming stronger. Your stop limit hasn't triggered. Then the stock begins to rise.

After a while, your ESP monitoring shows the stock's ESP score suddenly drops to 7, with the technical score in negative territory. Clearly the stock still appears to be a long term buy, but a period of short term weakness is clearly indicated. So you sell, just before the stock price falls through the floor.

Section Review

- For a buy signal to be in place, both fundamental and

113

technical scores must be positive.

- If the technical score then turns negative, be wary of short term weakness and sell.

- If the fundamental and the technical scores are both negative, then avoid the stock.

- Continually monitor, building the scorecard each day when it suits you (best after the market close).

- A changing ESP score will pre-warn of a possible impending change in price trend.

- The ESP Score needs to be positive for a buy signal, and the closer it is to maximum the stronger the buy signal.

- The ESP Score does not need to be negative for a sell signal (if you hold stock), but the closer to minimum it is the stronger the sell signal.

- Stocks that are trading with a high negative score, and where this score begins to move better, could be stocks to watch for a large positive share price movement in the near future. Changing fundamentals may bring in long term buyers and promote short term share price strength.

That really is it. Possibly the most comprehensive and yet easy stock picking and directional trading system you'll ever come across. But then, in the pursuit of profits, I've never believed in making things more complicated than they need to be.

PRACTICE MAKES PERTECT

Okay, so now I've given you all the knowledge you need to make your stock trading ESP a reality you can get started. But it may be that you've never traded stocks before so are a little reticent to start immediately. And that's fine, because apart from anything else you'll want to hone the system to your individual technique and ability.

Of course, if you are new to the trading and investment business you may still be a little reticent. But you don't have to be, because now I'm going to show you a couple of great online trading brokers that allow you to trade in a virtual environment, testing the ESP system and your individual ESP strategy.

TradeMONSTER

TradeMonster was formed in 2008 and claims to be 30% lower in its charging structure than other online brokers. It started as an options broker, but now covers stocks as well. It's easy to open an account, and once you've done this you can use its paperTrade application to not only learn how the ESP system can work for you, but also how to input and execute all the orders you need to utilize to make the best use of ESP.

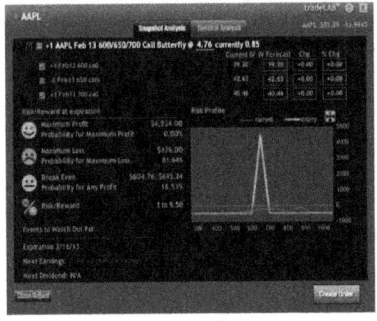
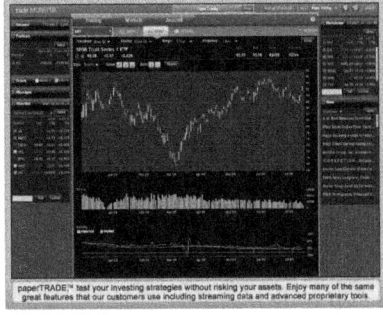

Interactive Brokers

IB has a great long term record, and also offers a huge range of international markets if you want to look further afield. It's an easy to use system, offering one click trading if you want (which makes position closing and opening fast and efficient). One thing that's really good about this system is that if an order gets executed and you don't have the funds in your account to execute other outstanding orders they will all be cancelled – this helps stop over trading.

It's got a great charting tool and a chat facility that allows you to talk to other traders. Best of all it has a PaperTrader system that allows you to trade in real time without committing actual money. You can test your strategies and make sure they work before placing your money into the market.

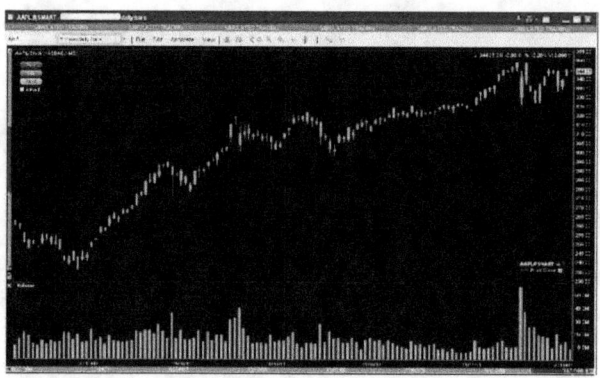

Of course, there are plenty of other online brokers available, and it may be that you decide to use none of these two before exploring other options. But these are two great online brokers, with whom it's easy to sign up with and that you can use all the order types that you'll need to successfully trade ESP.

You now have all the information you need to perfect your ESP trading strategy and move toward that four hour million. It's now down to you.

www.ingramcontent.com/pod-product-compliance
Lightning Source LLC
Chambersburg PA
CBHW060146200526
45165CB00023B/961